The Sea

Other titles in the Exploring Play series

Flight
Sue Sheppy
1-84312-288-X

Water
Carolyn Hewitson
1-84312-344-4

Woodland Creatures
Helen Shelbourne
1-84312-291-X

Ourselves
Helen Shelbourne
1-84312-290-1

Transport
Helen Shelbourne
1-84312-297-9

Bears
Helen Shelbourne
1-84312-294-4

Mini-Beasts
Carolyn Hewitson
1-84312-292-8

Rainforest
Sue Sheppy
1-84312-293-6

The Weather
Helen Shelbourne
1-84312-295-2

The Sea

Sue Sheppy

 David Fulton Publishers

David Fulton Publishers Ltd
The Chiswick Centre, 414 Chiswick High Road, London W4 5TF

www.fultonpublishers.co.uk

First published in Great Britain in 2006 by David Fulton Publishers

10 9 8 7 6 5 4 3 2 1

Note: The right of Sue Sheppy to be identified as the author of this work has been asserted by her in accordance with the Copyright, Designs and Patents Act 1988.

David Fulton Publishers is a division of Granada Learning, part of ITV plc.

Copyright © Sue Sheppy 2006

British Library Cataloguing in Publication Data
A catalogue record for this book is available from the British Library.

ISBN: 1-84312-289-8

Typeset by FiSH Books, London
Printed and bound in Great Britain

Contents

The author

Sue Sheppy is currently an independent educational consultant and trainer, who specialises in the Early Years. She has written a wide variety of project outlines for *Nursery World* magazine, drawing on her mainstream teaching experience and language support work for young bilingual pupils, both as a teacher and as a teacher adviser for Lancashire County Council. For a number of years now she has provided professional development for teachers and assistants across the whole of the Foundation Stage Curriculum, and dealt with a variety of issues around ethnic minority achievement, cultural diversity and equal opportunities. She keeps abreast of current research and practice in a variety of settings through her work as a Distance Education tutor for the University of Birmingham's Master of Education course in Bilingualism in Education.

Acknowledgements

The author and series editor would like to thank the children, parents and staff at:

- Broomhill Infants School, Brislington, Bristol
- The Nursery and Reception class, Wadebridge County Primary School, Wadebridge, Cornwall
- Happy Days Day Nursery, Wadebridge, Cornwall
- Snapdragons Nursery, Weston, Bath, Somerset
- Snapdragons Nursery, Grosvenor, Bath, Somerset
- Tadpoles Nursery, Combe Down, Bath, Somerset

for allowing us to take photographs of their excellent provision, resources and displays.

Also thank you to John, Jasmine, Eva and Alfie for their help throughout the series, and to Nina, Margaret and Ben at David Fulton Publishers for their patience, enthusiasm and support.

The Sea acknowledgements

This project has caused me to recall many happy childhood memories of summer holidays by the sea; in particular, those spent in the Isle of Wight, a favourite family haunt.

I express my thanks to those who took a number of the photographs included in this book, especially my husband, Paul, and Bernard Sparks. Thanks, too, to those who feature, especially Claire, Justin, Bella and Micah.

Introduction

For some people the sea is part of their daily life, for others a place of holiday.

Some people live close to the sea, while others have never seen it. It arouses strong feelings of joy, of fear, of respect and the children will be captivated by this exhilarating theme. The individual topics alliterate with the sea. They are seashore, shell, seagull, ship, shark and seal. Each separate topic will generate interesting projects for the children to explore, stimulating their creativity and their imagination, even if a visit to the seashore is not possible for your setting. In their play, the children will be continually developing their basic skills through the use of a whole range of resources including malleable and natural materials. Some of the equipment needed for construction will be provided by the practitioners, but the children will enjoy collecting other materials themselves such as shells, seaweed and pieces of driftwood, even if this has to be second-hand from friends and relatives. Models, photographs and books from home can also make important contributions to the display, which will stimulate further topic activities, as well as provide a record of achievement.

As the theme develops, the children will be stimulated to:

- develop their imaginative skills through role play;
- devise their own stories as they develop dialogues and create their own characters;
- count and match in a natural context;
- discover that others have alternative ways of viewing the world and learn to respect those differences.

The sea is a topic that will encourage the children to respond with their whole bodies, exploring the need for stillness to observe a crab scuttling across the sand, as well as experiencing the exhilaration of running along the water's edge with the wind blowing their hair. They will be invigorated by the salty taste of the ocean in their noses and on their lips, and will feel the excitement of clambering over rocks and exploring the back of dark damp caves. Seaside scenes may need to be simulated using the sandpit and the water tray, but still all the children's senses will need to be alert to see, to listen, to touch, to taste and to smell, and to begin to be aware of the need, sometimes, to interpret these experiences for others.

Activities suggested in each topic will be linked to the Early Learning Goals as identified in the *Curriculum Guidance for the Foundation Stage* (2000). In this way you will be able to monitor the areas of learning that the children are engaging in and ensure that they are accessing a full and balanced curriculum. As always, health and safety is the particular responsibility of the practitioner in the setting and, where appropriate, such issues are highlighted.

There are six topics in all, and these can each be used on a weekly basis for a half-term theme, or each over two weeks to cover the whole term. At other times, you may wish to use individual topics with another theme; for example, the ship might fit into a transport theme, or the seagull into a theme on flight. Alternatively, the children may become so absorbed in one of the topics that it is developed further, and becomes a major theme of its own. The seashore also provides an interesting environment to compare with life in the country or in an industrial town.

Each chapter has a book bank, which includes information and story books, and, where applicable, useful addresses and websites. Introducing a specific story to a theme can help children to focus on a particular aspect of the sea and to experience it through the eyes of the different characters. For example, using the book *Kipper's Beach Ball* (page 10) enables the children to relive the experience of the beach through the eyes of Kipper and enjoy their own games with a beach ball. Each chapter of this book suggests an ideal story to use as an activity. You may have an alternative you would prefer to use. The key point to remember is that, when using a story as the basis for an activity, you will need to have an identifiable aim. Also, alongside any creative and physical opportunities the activity provides, there is always the need to consider the consolidation and extension of language and thinking skills.

Each topic aims to help practitioners to provide learning opportunities for the children that are relevant, realistic and challenging, so that the diverse needs of all the children will be met and they will achieve their full potential. If the children's imagination is captured, then their learning will be speedier and more profound.

Links to the Foundation Stage Curriculum for the general theme of the sea

CLL Extend their vocabulary, exploring the meanings and sounds of new words.

KUW Ask questions about why things happen and how things work.

PD Handle tools, objects, construction and malleable materials safely and with increasing control.

General preparation

➤ In order to stimulate the children's interest and encourage investigation, set up an interactive area in the setting where observation tanks can be displayed and models and mobiles can be added as the topic develops.

● Because of the nature of this topic, what happens 'in the water' and 'on the sand' will be of prime importance, so the space for the topic focus must be chosen carefully to allow for water and sand to be safely, yet accessibly displayed.

● There will need to be table surfaces available to facilitate close-up observations, as well as to provide for the display of pertinent books, and the children's work.

- Posters, pictures and friezes could be used as the background to the display, so wall space would be helpful too. Digital photographs and paintings can be added as the topic progresses.

- Information books on all aspects of the sea could be displayed from the beginning, and other related stories added as each particular topic is introduced.

➤ Role play areas will need to be established later at the appropriate stage.

➤ Computers, tape recorders, video and digital cameras could provide resources for both practitioners and children to draw on. They can also contribute to the record keeping, alongside the traditional, and equally important, pencil and paper notes.

General activity content

1 Invite the children to share their own experiences of the sea, as either participants or observers. Ask open-ended questions to find out how much knowledge and understanding they already have about the topic. You could usefully record their responses pictorially, or verbatim, on a large sheet of paper to form a concept map. Group the information as the children respond, and note if they make any links themselves in their thinking. For example, if someone says *a fish*, others might begin to give the names of different types of fish, which you could record in a list under the fish heading. Someone else might contribute *seal* and say that fish and seal are linked because they both swim in the sea. Recording the children's chain of thought can be very helpful in discerning their conceptual development. If you have bilingual pupils in your group, accept labels in other languages. These can be written phonetically and the correct form added later with help from bilingual assistants, parents or members of the community.

2 Stimulate initial interest by looking at the information books on the topic during whole-group sessions with the children.

3 Share stories that relate to the theme, and encourage the children to play out their stories through role play, using the visual aids provided for the initial storytelling sessions. These could be life-size or model items, pictures, dressing-up clothes, masks or construction toys for the children to create their own properties.

4 As the display develops, encourage the children to interact with the items as appropriate.

Home–setting links

- Involve the parents and carers right from the beginning as this could promote a very productive exchange of ideas and resources.

- Provide information about the overall theme and each new topic area as it is introduced.

- Encourage contributions to the display, follow-up activities at home, library visits and opportunities to share pertinent experiences with the children.

● Make use of those who offer first-language support for children learning English as an Additional Language, who could tell stories to all the children. Be aware that some children might have had family or friends lost in tidal waves or boating accidents, and most children will have been aware of the tsunami disaster at the end of 2004, and seen its effects on television. For some the beach will have taken on a more sinister aspect that might need talking through with the children.

Key vocabulary

sea	seagull
sand	ship
seaweed	shark
seashore	seal
shell	

Health and safety

● When taking the children on trips, observe the legal regulations regarding the appropriate adult:child ratio; for preschool children this is one adult to two children.

● Adopt a routine with the children of washing their hands after they have been collecting natural resources including small creatures (as in activity on page 8).

● Careful supervision is always needed when the children are using plastic bin liners of any kind (as in activities on pages 31 and 45) that could be pulled over their heads.

● When visiting the beach or any outdoor venues, make sure the children wear hats and T-shirts if it is hot, and have sweaters and rainwear in case of a change in the weather.

● When near water, whether it be the sea, a boating lake or a paddling pool, make sure that all the adult supervisors are particularly alert. Check for coastguard and first-aid facilities in areas outside your setting. If you take the children on a boat, they should each be provided with a life jacket. Only adults should be involved in boiling water in a pan; the children must remain at a safe distance (as in activity on page 32).

● When children are tasting food, be aware of any allergies that they might have. If they are trying a certain food for the first time, always give them a small amount and be alert for any adverse reactions. Be aware, too, that some children might have to adhere to certain dietary requirements because of culture or religious faith.

Reference

DfEE (2000) *Curriculum Guidance for the Foundation Stage*. QCA.

Seashore

Links to the Foundation Stage Curriculum

Follow-up Activities

Home—setting Links

Seashore

Extending Learning

Resources and Preparation

Activity Content

Adult-led focus activities

1 Observation

The seashore is a fascinating place for the children to visit. There are so many different sounds and smells and sights for them to experience. Providing sensible precautions are taken in terms of safety issues, then the trip could prove to be a stimulating one for a whole scheme of work. Alternatively, your home-made seaside could be a fun place to explore through the use of imaginative sand and water activities.

◆ **Links to the Foundation Stage Curriculum**

MD   Show curiosity and observation by talking about shapes, how they are the same or why some are different.

KUW   Examine objects and living things to find out more about them.

> **Adult:child ratio 1:3 for sand area observation; 1:2 for a trip to the seashore**

◆ **Resources**

- ✔ A seashore
- ✔ Outdoor sandpit and/or indoor sand tray
- ✔ Magnifying glasses
- ✔ Binoculars
- ✔ Copy of *On the Seashore* by Anna Milbourne or any other information book about life at the seaside (see Book bank, page 19)
- ✔ Paper and pencils and/or a small handheld tape recorder (for recording notes)
- ✔ Digital camera

◆ **Preparation**

> Make a preparatory visit to your nearest suitable beach for the children in your setting. Inspect the shoreline for rock pools, sand dunes, sand, shells and pebbles, small caves, as well as facilities such as toilets. Check out the proximity of the coastguard, lifeboat station and first-aid services in case of emergencies. Plan the activities before the main trip, bearing in mind changes in the weather. Check the tides, as nothing would be more disappointing than arriving with a group of children eager to dig in the sand, only to find the sea is covering the whole beach, or conversely is

so far out that the children would have to walk miles to paddle in the sea, or even find a rock pool. Look up the bye-laws to see if it is against the law to remove any materials from the beach.

➤ Arrange a date for the visit and make the booking with your transport providers.

Home–setting links

● Write letters to the parents and carers about any trips to make it clear what is happening and what is needed in terms of funds, food and offers of support on the trip.

● Let the parents and carers know about the sea topic from the beginning and encourage them to take the children to the library to look for books about sea creatures, both in the sea and along the shore.

● If your children live in close proximity to the sea, ask parents to encourage the children to keep a diary to record sightings of sea creatures on family visits to the beach. The record can be pictorial and/or have a written description, which the adults and children can create together.

➤ Prepare your outdoor sandpit and/or indoor sand tray with fresh sand and begin to collect resources for use throughout the topic.

➤ Gather together all the other resources identified above.

➤ Put together a sea book box (see Book bank, page 19).

➤ On the trip to the seashore, decide how and when the digital camera is to be used. For example, will the children be shown how to use the camera and have easy access to it, or will the adults keep control of the camera and accompany the children while they take a photograph, or will the adults take the pictures at the children's request.

Activity content

1   Refer to the concept map of the sea (see page 3) and see if the children can identify items to do with the *landscape* of the beach, for example, the waves, the sand, the sand dunes, the rocks and rock pools, the caves and cliffs, pampas grass, seaweed. Show the book *On the Seashore* by Anna Milbourne or the information book of your choice. When the various items have been identified, circle them on the concept map for the children to see. The children will probably identify other items such as shells and starfish, but these have a section on their own later on so, although they should be acknowledged, they need not be dwelt on at any length in this first session.

2   Read the story of *Fergus the Sea Dog* by Tony Maddox, which will reinforce the landscape of the seashore, as shown in one of the information books (see Book bank, page 19).

3   Talk with the children about Fergus's experiences at the seaside and help them to think about the differences from his life at home on the farm. If your setting is in the town, it would be useful to have a copy of *Fergus the Farmyard Dog* (see Book bank, page 20) to help the children draw comparisons.

4   Make your visit to the beach, drawing on the expertise of the local residents and your knowledge of the particular area from your preparatory visit, to decide

what resources to take. The distance you have to travel will determine whether this is a full day trip or a morning or afternoon session. There will be implications for packed lunches, but snacks and drinks will be necessities. Sunblock, hats and T-shirts will be necessary on a hot day; warm jumpers and rainwear if the weather is cooler and unsettled.

5   Leave plenty of time for the children to experience the sensations of digging in the sand and of paddling in the sea with the sounds of waves crashing onto the beach and seagulls squawking overhead.

6   Even if the bye-laws disallow anything being removed from the beach, the children can still make a collection of items to view during their visit, such as shells, pebbles, seaweed, bits of driftwood, starfish. Hopefully, it will be a clean beach where cans and bottles and plastic bags are not strewn around; but the importance of keeping the beach free of litter can be a talking point with the children, anyway.

7   Talk with the children about the need to be very quiet when coming to observe sea creatures in the sand or in a rock pool, so as not to frighten them. Help the children to imagine how big and noisy they must seem to a tiny crab and how some creatures will withdraw into their shell if they feel afraid. The children might use fishing nets to examine these creatures more closely. Talk about safety issues to prevent anyone being nipped by a crab's claw.

8   Show the children how to use the shatterproof magnifying glasses for close-up work and the binoculars for more distant observations. Make sure that these are available for the children to use so they can observe any of the sea creatures they discover, watch the seagulls flying or look at small boats and ships out at sea.

9 Encourage the children to record their observations by speaking into the tape recorder, drawing a picture, making notes or by taking a photograph (if the procedure for this has been agreed, see page 7). Transcriptions of the tape recordings and prints of the photographs could then be added to the display.

Extending learning

Key questions

Q What can you see on the beach? What is the sea like? What colour are the waves? Is the sand soft and dry, or hard and wet? Are there any caves? Or rocks? Or dunes? Or cliffs?

Q What can you see on the sand or in the rock pool?

Q What does it look like? What shapes can you see? What colours? Are there any special patterns? Are they repeated?

Q What does it feel like? Is it hard? Or spiky? Does it scratch? Does it nip?

Q Is it alive? What is it doing? Is it resting? Is it burrowing into the sand?

Q What does it like to eat? Where can you find out?

Q How does it move? Can you walk sideways like a crab? How is your body different from a crab? Or a starfish?

Q What did Fergus discover before he met his new friend?

Q Where did he play with his friend? What happened when they went on the boat? What did Fergus feel like? Have you ever felt afraid? What did you wish for?

Key vocabulary

beach	sand	bucket
rock pools	fishing boat	spade
dark caves	seal	fishing net
crabs	giant waves	seaweed
seagulls	storm	

Follow-up activities

- Display different items from the children's beach collection on the sand (or model versions on a table back in the classroom). Encourage all the children to try to memorise the items. Then a towel is thrown over them and the children take turns to try to recall the items. Alternatively, or afterwards, the items are uncovered and one child turns away from the group and closes his or her eyes while someone else removes one item and hides it behind his or her back. The children in the group then ask, 'What's missing?' and the child turns round and looks at the items, and tries to identify which one is missing. The children take it in turns to hide their eyes and to remove an item.

- Pictures of the above items can be displayed next to their silhouettes for the children to match up (for examples see Photocopiable sheet 1).

- Books and poems about the seashore could be on the display, or in the sea book box, for children to look at any time. Practitioners and/or parents and carers could record some of these stories on tape for the children to listen to through headphones. If you have a junction box attached to your tape recorder, you could let several children listen at the same time. Children who speak more than one language could have tapes recorded bilingually.

■ Songs relating to the theme, such as, 'Oh, I Do Like to Be Beside the Seaside' (see Singing games and poems, page 20), could be sung in whole-group times, or tapes could be available for individuals to listen to through the headphones as above with the stories. Alternative words could be created to embrace the activities that the children like the most when they are *beside the sea*. For example:

> Oh, I do like to be beside the seaside
> Oh, I do like to be beside the sea
> Oh, I do like to run along the flat wet sand
> Where the wind blows strong and the seagulls land

◆ Home–setting link

Parents and carers could be encouraged to help in the search for songs, poems and stories. If you have any young bilingual learners, their parents or carers might also know appropriate rhymes or stories in their first language, which they could share with all the children.

2 Story: *Kipper's Beach Ball*

This activity enables the children to relive the experience of the beach through the eyes of Kipper and enjoy their own games with a beach ball.

◆ Links to the Foundation Stage Curriculum

CLL   Use a widening range of words to express or elaborate ideas.

PD   Negotiate space successfully when playing racing and chasing games with other children.

Adult:child ratio 1:8

◆ Resources

✔ Copy of *Kipper's Beach Ball* by Mick Inkpen (see Book bank, page 20)
✔ A story area were the children can sit comfortably
✔ A large clear space (inside or outside)
✔ Plastic beach balls to inflate
✔ Empty cornflake boxes
✔ Wind-up sharks, springing frogs, penguin rubbers to go on the end of pencils (or alternatives if these items cannot be replicated)

◆ Preparation

➤ Make sure that a large clear space is available at the time that you want it for your activity.
➤ Gather together the resources as identified above.

● Activity content

1   Recall the visit to, or discussion of, the beach and ask the children what they can remember.

2   Share the story *Kipper's Beach Ball* by Mick Inkpen. Draw the children's attention to the author's name. Some might notice that the name and the title of the story are printed in different colours. Ask them if they can see a pattern.

3   On page 1 (after the title page), talk to the children about the picture before reading the text on page 2. Ask them what they think is happening, and talk about their breakfast time and what they have to eat. See what they make of the *colourful wrinkly sort of thing* that fell into Kipper's bowl. See if anyone has ever collected items from a cereal packet. Read page 2 and turn over.

4   Read page 3. Have a look at the items that Tiger has collected. See if different children can identify the gifts on page 4. Make sure that the children are clear that 'Tiger' is really a dog. Ask the children why they think he is called 'Tiger'. Turn over.

5   Read page 5. See if the children can solve the puzzle before Tiger does. Turn over.

6   Read page 7. Ask the children what they think Kipper feels like now and how can you tell. Ask them what they think he will do next. Turn over.

7   Read pages 9 and 10. Give the children time to comment on the illustration and to share any of their own experiences of very bouncy balls. Turn over.

8   Ask the children where they think the dogs are and what they think will happen to the ball. Read page 12. Make sure that the children understand what a cliff is and return to a picture in an information book, if this is not clear. Talk to the children about how Kipper and Tiger could get down the cliff and onto the beach. Turn over.

9   Comment on the dogs coming down the cliffs. Read page 13. Talk about what the ball did: bouncing high on the hard sand, making the seagulls squawk, knocking the top off a sandcastle. You could return later to this page and consider the different words used to describe the actions of the ball: *circling* in the air, *dropped* onto the hard sand, *bounced up* again, *spinning* faster and faster, *rushed away*, *looped*, *skidded*. Turn over.

10   Read page 15. Look at page 16 and ask the children what they think will happen next. Turn over.

11   Read page 17. Ask the children why the writer said the wave looked like a seal. If they are unsure of what a seal looks like, remind them of the seals in *Fergus the Sea Dog*. Ask the children what they think will happen next. Turn over.

12   Read page 19. Ask the children what they think has happened, did they think the ball was safe, what caused the pop that Kipper heard. Turn over.

13 Read pages 21 and 22. Ask the children why they think Tiger suggested buying more cornflakes. Turn over.

14 Read page 23 and talk about page 24. Ask the children how Kipper got rid of all the cornflakes. Turn over.

15 Read page 25. Ask the children if they liked the story and whether they thought it was a happy or a sad one, and ask them why.

16 Put the story on the display table or in the sea book box so that the children can 'read' the story themselves and retell it to others, or choose it for practitioners to read to them again.

Extending learning

Key questions

Q Can you remember our trip to the beach? What did you see? What did you do? What did it feel like? What did it smell like?

Q Can you notice anything about the author's name and the title of the story? Is there a pattern? Does that pattern follow all the way through?

Q What do you think is happening here? What do you have for breakfast in the morning?

Q Have you ever collected gifts from a cereal packet? What did you find? What had Tiger found?

Q Is Tiger really a tiger? Why do you think he was called that? Do you think he looks fierce?

Q How can this wrinkly plasticky thing become a ball?

Q What do you think Kipper feels like now? How can you tell? What do you think he will do next?

Q Have you ever had a very bouncy ball? How did you play with it? Have you still got it at home? What happened to it?

Q Where do you think the dogs are? What do you think will happen to the ball? What is a cliff? Can you find one on this page? How do you think Kipper and Tiger could get down the cliff and onto the beach?

Q What did the ball do on the beach? Where did it finish up? What do you think will happen next?

Q Why do you think the writer said the wave looked like a seal? Can you see a seal in this picture? What do you think will happen to the ball?

Q What do you think has happened? Is the ball safe? What caused the pop that Kipper heard?

Q Why do you think Tiger suggested buying more cornflakes? How did Kipper get rid of all the cornflakes?

Q Did you like the story? Why? Why not? Was it a happy story? A sad one? Why is that?

Key vocabulary		
Kipper	cliff	frog
Tiger	beach	penguin
dogs	sea	wind-up shark
beach ball	waves	bounced
cornflakes		

Follow-up activities

- Provide some plastic beach balls for the children to blow up under supervision. Provide space indoors/outdoors as appropriate for bouncing, chasing, catching games. Arrange for some to be organised and some to be impromptu. An adult or child could stand in the centre of a circle and throw to each child in turn, who then throws the ball back to the centre. A net could be set up for two teams to play volleyball. Very young children need not play to any particular rules, but will enjoy trying to throw the ball over the net.

- Collect some used cornflake packets and a number of small items. Hide a different item in each packet. Play guessing games: Where is the...? What have you found? Is it the...? No, what is it?

- Have some cornflakes for snack time. Add fresh fruits cut up, or dried fruits such as apricots, dates or prunes. Seeds can also be added. For children with a milk allergy, fruit juices can be substituted. Some children might prefer the addition of yoghurt.

3 Creation of a beach

A sand tray will already have been established against the wall indoors under the sea display. An outdoor sandpit provides more scope for establishing a beach role play area for the children to act out stories, recall beach trips with the setting and/or with their families. Settings with a paddling pool already established can use this for the sea; otherwise, an inflatable paddling pool can be set up adjacent to/in the sandpit area.

Links to the Foundation Stage Curriculum

PD	Engage in activities requiring hand–eye coordination.
CD	Make three-dimensional structures.

Adult:child ratio 1:4

Resources

- ✔ Fresh sand, shells, pebbles, sticks, buckets, spades, dumper trucks, sieves
- ✔ Towels, sunblock, folding chairs, sunloungers, beach balls, sunhats, umbrella
- ✔ Boats, swimming costumes, goggles, fins, snorkel, plastic sea creatures of all kinds, waterweeds secured with large stones
- ✔ Café furniture and crockery, ice cream cones (models)
- ✔ Any other items identified by the children
- ✔ A large sheet of paper with a felt-tip pen

Preparation

➤ Gather the resources together.
➤ Decide on a date to begin the role play.
➤ Timetable seaside storytelling or poetry reading sessions each day.

Activity content

1 Read or tell several of the seashore stories or poems to the children on different days using material from the sea book box. Encourage them to recount the tales to stimulate their imagination before introducing the role play. Talk to the children about the characters in a particular story. Make a list of the properties needed and re-enact the story. Items needed could be drawn and labelled on a large sheet of paper and displayed to provide a prompt for the children.

2 Talk to them about the people they might want to introduce into their play: a fisherman or fisherwoman, an ice cream seller, someone to sell hot doughnuts, seaside rock or to run a café. Help the children decide what clothes and properties they might need to enact a particular story, or to create their own version.

3 Allow plenty of time for the children to create their own stories and try out new ideas.

4 Allow time for the children to enjoy the sensation of digging in the sand, making castles and moats. Allow some of the water to be used to form moats, and to provide areas of flat wet sand to make more stable models and to enable the children to bounce their beach balls successfully. The children can also write and draw pictures in wet sand.

Extending learning

Key questions

Q Who are the main characters? Can you tell us what happened in this story? What do the characters feel like? What makes them cross? Or happy? Or miserable?

Q Would you need any special clothes, or masks, to act out this story? What will you need to say?

Q Can you think of your own story? Who will be in your story? What will it be about?

Q How can you make the sand wet? What is different about the sand when it is wet? Or dry? What is dry sand best for? When is it better to use wet sand?

Q How will you carry your water? How will you mix it into the sand? What tools will you need? What is Jamie writing in the sand? What is Aisha drawing?

Key vocabulary	
sand	resting
beach	sandcastle
sea	bucket
water	spade
swimming	(as well as particular vocabulary
snorkelling	from the stories and poems)

Follow-up activities

- The children cover A4 sheets of activity paper with blue/green paint mixed with washing-up liquid to thicken it. They then use cardboard combs with a cut-out jagged edge to make wavy patterns to simulate the sea. The same process can be repeated with yellow paint to simulate the wavy patterns left on the beach when the tide is out.

- Sand pictures can be created by spreading strong glue onto an A4 sheet of activity paper and sticking shells and pebbles, bits of seaweed and driftwood onto the paper. A sheet of newspaper should be placed under paper. A mug of sand is poured over the picture and left until the glue has dried. The paper is then gently held up to allow any loose sand to fall onto the newspaper so that it can be recycled. The sand picture can be displayed as a contrast to the wavy pictures of the sea and the wet sand.

Encourage independent learning

Malleable materials

Additional resources

- ✔ Large sand tray
- ✔ Spades, buckets, rakes, combs, pastry cutters, pastry wheels
- ✔ Model vehicles, rubber animals
- ✔ Wooden tools

Possible activities/learning outcomes

KUW Begin to try out a range of tools and techniques safely.

Using the sand tray placed beneath the wall display of the sea, replenish this with fresh sand and dampen it slightly, so that the children can create sandcastles with the buckets and spades and race tracks for their model vehicles.

Leave rakes, combs, pastry wheels and cutters for the children to create patterns in the sand, and write and draw with the wooden tools.

The practitioner role

▲ Provide the children with the resources outlined above and encourage them to talk about any patterns they have created.

▲ Help them to succeed with their model making by encouraging them to talk through their plans with you. In this way, you can help them to clarify their thoughts and to reflect on what they have achieved.

▲ Provide any additional resources that the children need as their play develops.

Creative area

Additional resources

- ✔ Small and large tissue or sticky paper circles in a variety of bright colours
- ✔ Yellow A4 activity paper
- ✔ Glue, scissors
- ✔ Set of felt-tip pens, crayons

Possible activities/learning outcomes

CD Use ideas involving fitting, overlapping, in, out, enclosure, grids and sun-like shapes.

The children choose a size and colour(s) of tissue or sticky paper circles to overlap to create a colourful beach ball picture.

The circles need to be stuck onto a sheet of the yellow activity paper in such a way that they overlap but still retain their round shape. The children can experiment with folding the circles into halves and quarters.

The background can then be created with felt-tip pens, or with crayons, to set the ball in its context on the beach. The activity paper will simulate the sand, but waves, rocks and cliffs can be added.

The practitioner role

▲ Provide a range of appropriate materials for the children to make their beach ball pictures.

▲ Be ready to supply any additional resources that they might require.

▲ Support the children by encouraging them to talk about their ideas and the choices they are making about size, colour and shape.

▲ Talk to them about the effect created by overlapping the circles.

▲ Afterwards ask them if they are pleased with the result, or whether they would change anything next time.

Role play

Additional resources

✔ Choice of story book from the sea book box such as *Pirate Pete* by Kim Kennedy or *Duncan and the Pirates* by Peter Utton (see page 20) which refers to buried treasure and gives the children the opportunity to develop play with treasure chests, coins, sparkly necklaces and bangles, or gold and silver buttons

Possible activities/learning outcomes

CLL Use talk to organise, sequence and clarify thinking, ideas, feelings and events.

Fill the chest with treasure and bury it in the sand.

Use small-world figures to be the pirates arriving on the beach with their spades ready to dig up the treasure, or encourage the children to draw pirate faces on sticky labels, cut them out and stick them onto their fingertips to make puppets.

Develop new versions of the chosen story.

The practitioner role

▲ Re-read or retell the chosen story with the children.

▲ Talk to them about the plot, the characters and the parts that they like best.

▲ Ask about how the various characters feel at different times in the story and ask the children to share times when they have felt the same way.

▲ Support them as they talk through their plans and allow them space to develop their own ideas.

▲ Show the children how to create the sticky label puppets.

▲ Support the children to create their own versions of the story.

▲ Intervene only to move things on or to provide additional resources.

▲ Encourage the children to reflect on their play.

Book bank

Information books

On the Beach by Heather Amery and illustrated by Stephen Cartwright (2004). Usborne Publishing. ISBN 0746061846

Beachcombing: Exploring the Seashore by Jim Arnosky (2004). Dutton Children's Books. ISBN 0525471049. Non-fiction and fiction.

Summer Activity Book by Clare Beaton (1994). B Small Publishing. ISBN 1874735018 (5–9yrs). With a Press Out Windmill.

Sand (Four Corners Series) by Margaret Clyne and Rachel Griffiths (2004). Longman. ISBN 0582833736 (5–6yrs). Considers what sand is and what it is used for.

The Little Book of Sand and Water by Sally Featherstone and illustrated by Rebecca Savania (2002). Featherstone Education. ISBN 1904187528

The Living Seashore by N. Hester (2004). Franklin Watts. ISBN 0749656581

Seashore (First-hand Science) by Lynn Huggins-Cooper and illustrated by Shelagh McNicholas and David Burroughs (2004). Smart Apple Media. ISBN 1583404465

Seashore Sticker Book (Usborne Spotter's Guides Sticker Books) by C. King and J. Elliott (2004). Usborne Publishing. ISBN 074604769X

Into the A B Sea: Ocean Alphabet Book by Deborah Lee Rose and illustrated by Steve Jenkins (2000). Scholastic Press. ISBN 0439096960

Beach (Look and Say), model maker Jo Litchfield, design and illustration by Francesca Allen (2004). Usborne Books. ISBN 0746058691. Board book.

On the Seashore by Anna Milbourne and S. Gilder (2005). Usborne Publishing. ISBN 0746062397

Seashore (DK Eyewitness Books) by Steve Parker (2004). DK Publishing. ISBN 0756607205

By the Seashore (Nature Trail Books) (Touch and Feel Pages) by Maurice Pledger (1998). Silver Dolphin. ISBN 1571453229

Shapes on the Seashore (Band 2A Collins Big Cat Guided Reading Series) by Frances Ridley and illustrated by Ali Teo (2005). Collins Educational. ISBN 0007185561. Non-fiction and fiction.

Websites

Baker Ross: www.bakerross.co.uk

BBC: www.bbcshop.com

DKL Marketing: www.dkl.co.uk

Early Learning Centre: www.elc.co.uk

FEVA (UK): www.feva.co.uk

INGEB: www.ingeb.org

Mantra Lingua: www.mantralingua.com

Playmobil: www.playmobil.com

Wader Quality Toys UK: www.wadertoys.de

Story books

Olive's Pirate Party by Roberta Baker and illustrated by Debbie Tilley (2005). Little, Brown. ISBN 0316167924

The Sandcastle (BBC Balamory Series) (2004). Red Fox. ISBN 0099472864. Also available as DVD/video from www.bbcshop.com

Grandma's Beach by Rosalind Beardshaw (2002). Bloomsbury Publishing. ISBN 0747555540

The Berenstain Bears' Seashore Treasure (I Can Read Book) by Stan Berenstain (illlustrator) and Jan Berenstain (2005). HarperFestival. ISBN 006058341X

Seaside Bear (Photo Friends Series) by Steve Bland (2004). Campbell Books. ISBN 1405019891. Board book with pull-down mirror.

The Little House by the Sea (Red Fox Picture Books) by Benedict Blathwayt (1994). Red Fox. ISBN 0099293412

Abracadabra Abegail at the Seashore by Victoria Broussard (2004). Trafford Publishing. ISBN 1412039509

Miffy at the Seaside by Dick Bruna (1997). Egremont Books. ISBN 1405209852. Board book.

Where Is Maisy Going? (a Lift the Flap Surprise Book) by Lucy Cousin (2003). Walker Books. ISBN 074455764X

Stella, Star of the Sea by Marie-Louise Gay (1999). Groundwood Books. ISBN 0888993374

Katie Morag and the New Pier by Mairi Hedderwick (1997). Red Fox. ISBN 0099220822

Lucy and Tom at the Seaside by Shirley Hughes (1993). Puffin Books. ISBN 0140544593

Kipper's Beach Ball by Mick Inkpen (2004). Hodder Children's Books. ISBN 0340879017

Pirate Pete by Kim Kennedy and illustrated by Doug Kennedy (2002). Harry N. Abrams. ISBN 0810943565

I Saw a Ship a-Sailing by Sian Lewis and illustrated by Graham Howells (2001). Pont. ISBN 1859029086

Fergus the Farmyard Dog by Tony Maddox (1992). Barrons Juveniles. ISBN 0812017633

Fergus the Sea Dog by Tony Maddox (2004). Piccadilly Press. ISBN 1953407194

Just Grandma and Me (Golden Look-Look Book) by Mercer Mayer (illustrator) (2001). Golden Books. ISBN 0307118932

There's Always One! by John Prater (2004). Hodder Children's Books. ISBN 0340855347. Rabbits at the beach and one comes to the rescue of the others.

The Cat in the Hat Learning Library: Clam-I-Am! All About the Beach by Tish Rabe (2005). Random House. ISBN 0375822801

Yo Yo Goes to the Beach by Jeannette Rowe (2001). Southwood Books. ISBN 1903207347

Duncan and the Pirates by Peter Utton (2004). A & C Black. ISBN 0713667397

Singing games and poems

A sailor went to sea, sea, sea
To see what he could see, see, see;
But all that he could see, see, see
Was the bottom of the deep blue sea, sea, sea!

by Anon. in *This Little Puffin: A Treasury of Nursery Rhymes, Songs and Games* compiled by Elizabeth Matterson (1991). Puffin Books. ISBN 0140340483

Seaside Poems edited by Jill Bennett and illustrated by Nick Sharratt (1998). Oxford University Press. ISBN 0192761749

'Four Little Girls' by A.E. Dudley in *Happy Landings: Poems for the Youngest* (Zebra Books) edited by Howard Sergeant (1971). Evans Bros. ISBN 0237351897

'I Do Like to Be Beside the Seaside!' by John Glover-Kind (www.ingeb.org/folksong.html, accessed 15/08/2005)

'At the Seaside' by Robert Louis Stevenson in *Happy Landings: Poems for the Youngest* (Zebra Books) edited by Howard Sergeant (1971). Evans Bros. ISBN 0237351897

Equipment

Acrylic Jewels. A sparkling assortment of shiny-backed coloured jewels. Sizes 7mm–23mm. Sold in packs of 100 or 300. www.bakerross.co.uk Tel: 0870 241 1867

Pirates Treasure. A wooden three-dimensional pirate ship with treasure that children can lock together. www.dkl.co.uk Tel: 01604 678780 (2yrs +)

Lightweight Binoculars. Magnification to the factor of six. www.elc.co.uk Tel: 08705 352 352

Wooden Pirate Ship. With cannons, crow's nest, plank, helm, anchor and sail. Runs on wheels. Additional Pirate Sticker Set, Cannons, Pirate's Accessories Set and four-piece Pirate Outfit. www.elc.co.uk Tel: 08705 352 352 (3yrs +)

Glitter Gems. A jewellery box with a range of gems and glitter for making jewellery as well as paints and glue for decorating the box. www.feva.co.uk Tel: 01494 460900 (6–10yrs)

Seaside frieze illustrated by Louise Daykin, size 30cm x 150cm. www.mantralingua.com Tel: 020 8445 5123

Viking Longboat. A versatile toy that children can construct themselves with the crew and the rigging provided. www.playmobil.com Tel: 01268 490184 (4yrs +)

Baby Trucks. Can tip back and steer. www.wadertoys.de Tel: 01582 713943 (2yrs +)

2

Shell

Links to the Foundation Stage Curriculum

Follow-up Activities

Home–setting Links

Shell

Extending Learning

Resources and Preparation

Activity Content

Adult-led focus activities

1 Observation

Sea creatures such as crabs, lobsters, prawns, shrimps, cockles and mussels are called crustacea. Most of these crustacea have a hard crusty shell and several pairs of jointed legs. While some of these creatures like to live on the shore, others prefer deeper water. Crabs live in the sea and along the shore in rock pools. As they are sometimes found under rocks and seaweed, one or two will most likely have been discovered by the children on their trip to the beach. In the first activity, the children will be observing the abandoned empty shells of sea creatures that have been washed up on the beach. However, it is important that they realise that small sea creatures once inhabited these shells. Because these tiny creatures have the option of retreating into their shells and closing them tight shut at the least sign of danger, the children will be unable to observe many of these creatures in their active state. However, they will be able to view them emerging from their shells at very close quarters through video clips from nature programmes, such as those broadcast by David Attenborough for the BBC with hidden cameras. Here the shellfish can be seen moving and feeding freely (see Websites, page 33).

🔶 Links to the Foundation Stage Curriculum

MD Use terms such as *greater, smaller, heavier* or *lighter* to compare quantities.

KUW Look closely at similarities, differences, patterns and change.

CD Make constructions, collages, paintings, drawings and dances.

Adult:child ratio 1:8

🔶 Resources

✔ Video player and nature video clip (see Websites, page 33)
✔ Variety of shells of different sizes and shapes (see Websites, page 33)
✔ Balance
✔ Sorting trays
✔ Magnifying glasses
✔ Small handheld tape recorder
✔ Paper with writing and colouring implements

Preparation

➤ Book the video recorder.

➤ Programme a session for the children to watch a video clip of shellfish in action.

➤ Gather together the resources detailed above.

Home–setting links

● Let the parents and carers know about the shell topic from the beginning and encourage them to take the children to the library to look for books about shellfish, or to contribute any from home.

● A parent or carer might be willing to bring their own shell collection into the setting to show the children.

● Some parents might have cooked mussels at home and the children could have experiences to share of watching the shells open up in the boiling water. (see page 32)

➤ Arrange a time to view the video clip (see Websites, page 33).

Activity content

1 Refer to the concept map of the sea (see page 3) and see if the children can identify any living creatures that have shells. Appoint different children to circle the pictures and labels of the creatures they find with a coloured felt-tip pen.

2 Show the video clip of a shellfish laying its eggs, feeding, moving around and retreating into its shell when it senses danger.

3 Allow time for the children to share their own experiences. Some may have seen a crab, for example, on the recent beach trip. Allow them time to explain where they saw it. Find out if they caught it in their fishing net from a rock pool or whether it was hiding under some seaweed, or running across the sand.

4 Tip the bag of empty shells out onto the table. Encourage the children to examine them carefully: to feel them and smell them. Provide shatterproof magnifying glasses for close-up observations of the shells and encourage the children to draw some of the patterns they see.

5 Talk about whether the shells are rough or smooth, or a mixture of both. Ask the children if the outside of any of the shells scratched their hands and why they think some are rough like this. Others are very sharp along the edges; warn the children that they might cut their fingers and talk about why the fish have developed like this.

6 Put the sorting trays on the table and encourage the children to sort the shells into groups. Talk together about which criteria to choose first. It is possible to look at size, shape, pattern, colour or texture. Count the number of shells in the various groups. For older children try overlapping circles on the floor or tabletop to find shells that fall into two groups at the same time, for example, a shell could be small and spiky or thin and smooth.

7 Place the balance on the table and ask the children to predict which shells are heavier and which are lighter. Weigh the shells to see if they were right. Ask the children how many small shells they think will be needed to balance one big shell. Find out how many small shells are needed and then count them with the children. Help them to keep a pictorial record of the sum and to write the numbers.

Extending learning

Key questions

Q What was happening on the video? What did you see? How did they move?

Q Have you seen crabs running across the sand before? How do they move? Can you show us?

Q Can all shellfish run like that? Why not?

Q What do they like to eat?

Q How shall we sort out these shells? Which ones are greater? Which ones are smaller? Which ones are rough? Which ones are smooth? Which ones are both rough and smooth? Why is that? Which ones have a spiral pattern? Which ones are long and thin? Why are the shells different shapes and sizes?

Q Which shell do you think is heavier? Were you right? Which shell do you think is lighter? Were you right?

Q How many small shells are needed to balance this big one? Can you count them? Can you draw a picture of the sum? Can you write the numbers?

Key vocabulary		
shell	cockle	spiky
crab	mussel	heavier
lobster	seaweed	lighter
prawn	rough	greater
shrimp	smooth	smaller

Follow-up activities

■ Songs and rhymes about shellfish like this tongue twister, for example: 'She Sells Seashells on the Seashore', or 'Coral' by Christina Rossetti (see Singing games and poems, page 33).

■ Cook some shell-shaped pasta and eat it cold or hot for snack time with salad dressing or tomato sauce, as appropriate.

■ Place shells on activity paper for the children to draw around and to copy their colours and patterns, or make prints by gently placing thin paper over a shell, round side up, and making a rubbing using a coloured crayon.

2 Story: *Sharing a Shell*

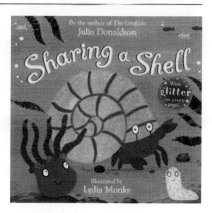

This activity is built round an engaging tale by Julia Donaldson, which is beautifully illustrated by Lydia Monks; there is glitter on every page. *Sharing a Shell* is based on factual information about the hermit crab, which has a very soft shell itself and so uses other creatures' discarded shells to hide in for protection. In this story we follow the exploits of a crab as he moves around trying to find a safe home and when he has found one is not happy, initially, about sharing it with anyone else.

● Links to the Foundation Stage Curriculum

PSE   Relate and make attachments to members of their group.

CLL   Describe main story settings, events and principal characters.

Adult:child ratio 1:8

● Resources

- ✔ Copy of *Sharing a Shell* by Julia Donaldson (see Book bank, page 33)
- ✔ Blue or green card
- ✔ Lollipop sticks
- ✔ Felt-tip pens and paint
- ✔ Brightly coloured A4 activity paper
- ✔ Scissors
- ✔ Large round buttons
- ✔ Pipe cleaners
- ✔ Sticky tape

● Preparation

- ➤ Acquire at least one copy of *Sharing a Shell* and arrange a time for the story session.
- ➤ Use an information book with a page on hermit crabs to introduce the session.
- ➤ Gather together the other resources to make the properties for the story.

● Home–setting link

Let the parents and carers know about the shell topic from the beginning and encourage them to take the children to the library to look for books about shellfish or to contribute any from home. A parent or carer might have photographs taken at the beach that they would be willing to share.

◆ Activity content

1   Refer to the concept map of the sea (see page 3) and see if the children can identify a living creature that has a shell. Ask the children to draw a circle around any that they find.

2   Read the story *Sharing a Shell* to the children several times. If you have bilingual children, arrange to have a staff member who speaks their first language, or a parent or carer, to read the story too, or to follow up with questions.

3   Encourage the children to describe the setting for the story, what happened and who the main characters are.

4   Encourage the children to talk about times when they had to learn to share something new and precious with other children. Ask them what they felt like and what were they worried about.

5   Encourage the children to think about times when they were glad to be with someone else. Perhaps they were frightened, or had been hurt or had got lost. Ask the children to share their experiences and to think of the importance of having friends who can enjoy happy and sad times with you.

6   Talk about how the little crab felt in the story when he was stung on the nose. Ask the children if they have ever been stung; ask them how it happened and what they did about it.

7   Make puppets on sticks with the children representing the main characters in the story. Each child in the group can draw a picture of one of the creatures using a felt-tip pen: the hermit crab, a blobby purple anemone, a tickly bristleworm, a whelk shell. These pictures need to be cut out and stuck onto blue or green card. The card is then cut to give a wavy edge to represent the water of a rock pool and then taped to a lollipop or balsa wood stick for the children to hold and re-enact the story (disposable wooden chopsticks from a Chinese or Thai takeaway are ideal).

◆ Extending learning

Key questions

Q   Who can find a creature with a shell on our map? What is it called? Can you draw a red circle round it?

Q   Who is the story about? What is happening? Does the little crab find a shell house?

Q   Who comes to share his shell? Is the crab happy about his visitors? Why not?

Q   Do you find it difficult to share sometimes? Why is that?

Q   Are there times when you have been glad someone else was there? Perhaps you were lost? Or frightened? Or lonely? Or hurt? Can you tell us what happened?

Q   How did the little crab feel at the end of the story? How do you feel when you have made a new friend?

Key vocabulary	
hermit crab	bristleworm
anemone	whelk shell

⬢ Follow-up activities

- The stick puppets should be made available for the children to use any time to act out the story, and to develop their own stories.

- The children can make their own pictures of shellfish using paint or collage. Large round buttons could be turned over and stuck onto the background to simulate shells and the creatures' legs could be drawn on with felt-tip pens, or the 'shell' could be raised up off the paper by using short lengths of pipe cleaner

- Print spiral shapes on A4 sheets of brightly coloured activity paper (see Photocopiable sheet 2). Encourage the children to cut carefully along the lines beginning at the outside edge and working their way into the centre. These shell-like shapes will make beautiful mobiles to hang over your sea display.

- Use the book *Toddlerobics: Animal Fun* by Zita Newcome (see Book bank, page 33). One of the movements is to scuttle like a crab.

- Have other stories and information books available about shellfish (see Book bank, page 33).

3 Seashell jewellery

In this activity the children make some jewellery using shell shapes and patterns to wear in the role play area and when acting out stories with merpeople and other sea stories. It is important that the jewellery is as individual as possible and that the children be given the freedom to design their own pieces. Support can be given in terms of the materials provided and in the talk that goes on around the activity.

⬢ Links to the Foundation Stage Curriculum

PSE   Be confident to try new activities, initiate ideas and speak in a familiar group.

CD   Experiment to create different textures.

Adult:child ratio 1:6

⬢ Resources

- ✔ Pictures, paintings, photographs or posters showing shells
- ✔ Shell-covered boxes, shell necklaces and/or bracelets, ornaments made of shells
- ✔ Clay and/or dough
- ✔ Uncooked tube pasta (macaroni, rigatoni, penne, ditali or cresta di gallo)
- ✔ Wooden tools
- ✔ Long coloured laces, shirring elastic, large round-ended darning needles
- ✔ Paints
- ✔ Hole puncher, hole reinforcements

⬢ Preparation

➤ *Home–setting link.* Ask the parents or carers if anyone has any shell-covered objects, ornaments made from shells that they would be willing to bring to show to the children or to lend to the display.

➤ Add the pictures of shells to the sea display (see page 2) and any ornaments or jewellery made from shells.

➤ Gather all the disposable resources together and make them available in separate containers.

➤ Cut lengths of shirring elastic ready to use for wrist and ankle bracelets.

➤ Make the paints and darning needles accessible to the children and show them how to thread the needles.

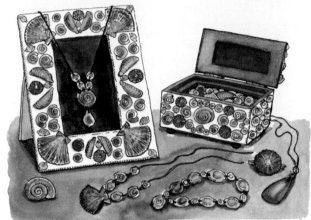

➤ Prepare the glue in suitable containers. Old film canisters are useful for strong glues, which need to be used sparingly, and they have a lid to cover the glue for storage.

➤ Provide large round-ended darning needles to thread the shirring elastic.

⬢ Activity content

1 First, look at the pictures of the shells with the children. This might require a walk over to the sea display, or to the book corner. Also examine carefully any shell jewellery, covered boxes or objects made with shells, which have been brought in by the children, their carers or the practitioners.

2 Talk about the characteristics of the shells, their size, their colour, what they have in common and what is different.

3 Talk through the way jewellery can be made with the items available.

4 To make a pendant, a small ball of clay or dough can be flattened slightly and a rounded shell pressed down to give its outer shape. The shell is then turned over and its rounded outer side is pressed into the clay/dough to provide the pattern. Talk about the choice of a shell and the need for a distinctive edge, a bold pattern and a rough texture; a cockleshell would work better than a smooth mussel shell, for example, because the pattern for an imprint needs to have high and low points.

5 The wooden tool is used to make a small hole in the top of the pendant, which is then left to dry. When it is dry, paint it and thread it with one of the coloured laces and tie the ends together to make the pendant.

6 To make a necklace or bracelet from pasta, thread each piece with the darning needle and the shirring elastic. When it is complete, tie up the ends and slip the necklace round the neck or place the bracelet round an ankle or a wrist.

⬡ Extending learning

Key questions

Q Can you tell me about this shell? What is it like? What shape is it? Does it look different from this one? How is it different? What things are the same?

Q Which shell will you choose for your pendant? What do we need to look for to make a clear print? Would this one be suitable? Why? Why not?

Q How can you make a hole in your pendant? Where will you put it? Why?

Q Will you make a necklace or a bracelet? Which shape will you choose for your shells? What do we call that shape? Do you want to change it?

Q Do you need any paints? Which colour do you want? What is it called? Do you want to add some more colours?

Q Do you want to make a pattern on your 'shell'? What could you use to do that?

Q How will you thread your pendant/necklace/bracelet?

Q Where will you wear this bracelet? Round your wrist or round your ankle?

Key vocabulary

pendant	pattern	lace
necklace	colour	elastic
bracelet	rough	hole
shells	smooth	thread
shape		

⬡ Follow-up activities

- Encourage the children to continue making their own jewellery using clay or dough and/or a variety of pasta shapes. Once they have been supported through the process, the children should be able to develop their own creations, which might include making earrings, which can be hung over the ears with shirring elastic.

- Encourage the children to use these pieces of jewellery in the role play area as they act out stories. The jewellery could be part of some buried treasure or belong to the wardrobe of the merpeople.

- Use a small rubber hermit crab, or encourage the children to draw a crab on some card and cut it out. Punch four holes on each side of the crab and reinforce them. Thread a short length of pipe cleaner through each hole on one side. Run it under the crab and up through the opposite hole to make eight legs in all. Ask the children to choose three to five large shells. One child hides the crab, while another hides his or her eyes and then guesses which shell it is under. Count the number of guesses each child takes before finding the crab.

- Related stories, rhymes and poems can be accessed from the Book bank (see page 33 for suggested titles).

Encourage independent learning

Creative area

Additional resources

- ✔ Small cardboard boxes
- ✔ Glue
- ✔ Small shells or uncooked pasta: conchiglie (shells)
- ✔ Tissue paper

Possible activities/learning outcomes

KUW Notice and comment on patterns.

To make jewellery boxes, provide small cardboard boxes.

Glue a number of small shells (or pasta alternative) onto the outside of the whole box or just the lid, depending on your resources, as decoration.

Choose a small amount of tissue paper, scrunch it up to make a cushion and place it in the bottom of the box.

Place the pendant or other item on the tissue paper and replace the lid.

The practitioner role

▲ Talk to the children about the need for jewellery boxes. Perhaps bring your own boxes to show the children.

▲ Look at any boxes or other items decorated with shells on the display table. Talk about the choices people have made and how they have arranged the shells and why.

▲ Recall any stories and poems you have read to the children about treasure. Help them to think about what the real treasure of the sea might be: the fish, the shellfish used for food, but also the beautiful colours, rich patterns and beautiful shapes of the shells. Talk about the need to keep the sea clean so that these tiny creatures can continue to live.

Malleable materials

Additional resources

- ✔ Clay
- ✔ Twigs, leaves
- ✔ Ferns
- ✔ Moss
- ✔ Pieces of cut-up black plastic bin liners
- ✔ Shells
- ✔ Water
- ✔ Aluminium foil
- ✔ Stones
- ✔ Cocktail sticks
- ✔ Sticky tape
- ✔ Gravel or wood chippings

Possible activities/learning outcomes

PD Explore malleable materials by patting, stroking, squeezing, pinching and twisting them.

Make a garden to associate with the rhyme:

> Mary, Mary, quite contrary
> How does your garden grow?
> With silver bells and cockleshells
> And pretty maids all in a row

Cover a flat board with a layer of clay, leaving a winding pathway through.

Scoop some clay out to form a small pond and line with the black plastic bin liner (see page 4).

Place stones round the top to hold down the liner.

Press some small shells into the clay.

Place the moss over the rest of the clay and stick in pieces of ferns to act as foliage.

Make bell shapes from folded pieces of aluminium foil and attach these to cocktail sticks at one end with sticky tape.

Stand the sticks upright into the clay.

Pour a little water into the pond.

Put gravel or wood chippings along the path.

If the children wish, they can place a house at one end of the path, which can be made out of Lego, or an old shoebox with a dried grass or straw roof to look like a thatched cottage.

Other items can be added, such as ducks swimming on the pond, fish or frogs in the water, pieces of weed trailing in the water, play people gardening.

The practitioner role

▲ Say the rhyme: 'Mary, Mary, Quite Contrary' with the children, teaching it to them if they do not know it.

▲ Look at the basic resources and talk through possible ways of using them. The children might have different ideas from the suggestions above and these need to be taken account of.

▲ Be prepared to collect additional items that the children might identify.

▲ Introduce and encourage the children to use the vocabulary of manipulation, such as *press*, *squeeze*, *bend*, *smooth out*, *shape*, *roll*, *flatten*.

▲ Support the children's mathematical language by encouraging them to count out the shells and the silver bells. Talk about the ordering, whether the bells and shells are to be placed alternately, two to one, in a particular shape or at random.

Role play

Additional resources

✔ Shells

✔ Stall

✔ Cooker, pan, plates, wooden forks

✔ Vinegar bottle

✔ Sticky tape

Possible activities/learning outcomes

CD Use available resources to create props to support role play.

Try to say the tongue twister

> She sells seashells on the seashore;
> The shells that she sells are seashells I'm sure.
> So if she sells seashells on the seashore,
> I'm sure that the shells are seashore shells.

(See Singing games and poems, page 33.)

Dress up a shellfish seller with an apron.

Provide a stove from the home area and a pan containing shellfish.

Make the cockles and mussels with dough, place each one in two matching shells taped together and put them in the pan.

Set up a stall with shellfish to sell and some vinegar for the customers to put on their food.

The seller can open up each shell to show that it has been cooked, and place the cockle or mussel on a customer's plate. The shellfish can be served in their shells.

Give each customer a wooden fork to eat their shellfish.

The practitioner role

▲ Talk about the difference between empty shells and those with the sea creatures still inside. In the rhyme we do not know if the woman is selling shellfish or empty shells.

▲ See if any of the children have eaten shellfish and can share their experience. A number may have eaten crab or scampi, but a few may have tried mussels, cockles or even oysters. The practitioner might decide to cook some mussels to show the children how the shells open up in boiling water. Clearly, there are safety issues here. First, the children will need to be kept at a safe distance from the boiling water (see page 4), but the practitioner could lift the shellfish up with tongs at different stages. Then if the food is to be tasted, permission should be sought from the parents and carers, and careful attention paid to any allergies the children might have to shellfish (see page 4).

▲ Stimulate the children's imagination by reading and telling stories and rhymes about sea creatures to enable them to gain confidence in constructing their own narratives.

Book bank

Information books

The Little Book of Sand and Water by Sally Featherstone and illustrated by Rebecca Savania (2002). Featherstone Education. ISBN 1904187528

The Living Seashore by N. Hester (2004). Franklin Watts. ISBN 0749656581

A Rockpool on the Seashore (Life in a   Series) by Sally Morgan (2004). Chrysalis Children's Books. ISBN 1841389404

Read and Learn: Sea Life by Lola M. Schaefer (2004). Raintree. ISBN 1844210197

Seashore Buddies (Scrub-a-Dub Series) (2005). Chrysalis Children's Books. ISBN 1844584720. Rag book, non-fiction and fiction.

Websites

Amazon: www.amazon.co.uk (*Shell* video from the Dorling Kindersley Eyewitness Series using special effects)

Baker Ross: www.bakerross.co.uk

BBC: www.bbcshop.com Nature videos, for example, *The Blue Planet* and *Deep Blue*.

BIG Spielwarenfabrick: www.big.de

Early Learning Centre: www.elc.co.uk

FEVA (UK): www.feva.co.uk

Library Video: www.libraryvideo.com *Sea Animals* is narrated by the baby animals themselves including a hermit crab.

Shells-a-Plenty: www.shellsaplenty.com These shells are priced in dollars, but can be purchased with a credit card, or you might find a more local outlet.

TOLO Toys: www.tolotoys.co.uk

Wader Quality Toys UK: www.wadertoys.de

Story books

The Little House by the Sea (Red Fox Picture Books) by Benedict Blathwayt (1994). Red Fox. ISBN 0099293412

Mermaids (Touchy-Feely Board Books Series) by S. Cartwright and F. Watt and illustrated by G. Bird (2004). Usborne Publishing. ISBN 074605663X

Sharing a Shell by Julia Donaldson and illustrated by Lydia Monks (2005). Macmillan Children's Books. ISBN 1405020482

Toddlerobics: Animal Fun by Zita Newcome (2000). Walker Books. ISBN 074457787X

Platypus by Chris Riddell (2001). Viking Children's Books. ISBN 0670894206. Platypus collects a shell not realising a crab still lives in it.

Singing games and poems

'She Sells Seashells on the Seashore' by Anon. in *100 Nursery Rhymes* selected by Anne McKie and illustrated by Ken McKie (1994 edition). Ladybird Books. ISBN 0721417183

Seaside Poems edited by Jill Bennett and illustrated by Nick Sharratt (1998). Oxford University Press. ISBN 0192761749

'Coral' by Christina Rossetti in *Happy Landings: Poems for the Youngest* (Zebra Books) edited by Howard Sergeant (1971). Evans Bros. ISBN 0237351897

Equipment

Acrylic Jewels. A sparkling assortment of shiny-backed coloured jewels. Sizes 7mm–23mm. Sold in packs of 100 or 300. www.bakerross.co.uk Tel: 0870 241 1867

Mini Sticky Sea Creatures. Throw them at any surface and they will crawl down and return to their original shape and size. Assorted designs. www.bakerross.co.uk Tel: 08702411867 (5yrs +)

Big Diggi Sandy. Designed to fit into a sandpit. Dredging shovel easy to use and can move a lot of sand. www.big.de Tel: 01296 662992 (3yrs +)

Coral-like Bracelets. Can be purchased relatively cheaply from outlets such as British Home Stores to add to the role play accessories.

Collage Set of Mirrors and Beads. www.elc.co.uk Tel: 08705 352 352 (3yrs +)

Collage Set of Small Shells. www.elc.co.uk Tel: 08705 352 352 (3yrs +)

Duplo Team Construction Dumper Truck and Digger. www.elc.co.uk Tel: 08705 352 352 (2–5yrs)

Push 'n' Go Crab. www.elc.co.uk Tel: 08705 352 352 (6mths +)

Glitter Gems. A jewellery box with a range of gems and glitter for making jewellery as well as paints and glue for decorating the box. www.feva.co.uk Tel: 01494 460900 (6–10yrs)

Kelvin the Activity Crab. www.tolotoys.co.uk Tel: 02380 662600 (birth +)

Baby Trucks. Can tip back and steer. www.wadertoys.de Tel: 01582 713943 (2yrs +)

3

Seagull

Links to the Foundation Stage Curriculum

Follow-up Activities

Home–setting Links

Seagull

Extending Learning

Resources and Preparation

Activity Content

Adult-led focus activities

1 Observation

The screeching cry of the seagull is strongly associated with the seashore, but these birds are often to be found inland feeding on open fields and swimming in freshwater lakes. The larger herring gulls can also be found feeding at rubbish tips. In the first activity, the children recall their observation on their beach trip of seagulls in flight and walking on the seashore, but are also asked to look out for seagulls in the local fields as they feed. A visit to the local park may also provide an opportunity to observe these familiar birds. It is unlikely that the children will be able to view baby seagulls emerging from their nest at very close quarters, as gulls' nests are mostly situated on cliff tops, or on roof tops in coastal towns, but video clips from nature programmes, such as those broadcast by David Attenborough for the BBC with hidden cameras, can show the process very clearly and safely. The BBC often has a webcam link where seagulls can be observed at various stages of development (see Websites, page 48).

Links to the Foundation Stage Curriculum

PSE   Maintain attention, concentrate and sit quietly when appropriate.

KUW   Observe, find out about and identify features in the place they live and the natural world.

Adult:child ratio 1:2 for a park visit; 1:8 for a video clip

Resources

✔ Local park with a lake
✔ Video player and nature video clip
✔ Binoculars
✔ Small handheld tape recorder
✔ Digital camera
✔ Paper with writing and colouring implements

Preparation

➤ Arrange for a visit to a local park after making a preliminary visit to inspect the facilities and to find out if there are any appropriate activities already provided for the age group of your children. If not, devise some of your own before the main trip.

➤ Arrange a date for a visit and, if you wish to make use of the local experts, make a booking with the park ranger. Book your transport providers if necessary.

Home–setting links

- Write letters to the parents and carers about the trip to make it clear what is happening and what is needed in terms of funds, food and offers of support on the trip. You might want to reverse the order of the first two activities to include the preparation of a picnic stimulated by the story of *The Lighthouse Keeper's Lunch* (see Activity 2).

- Let the parents and carers know about the seagull topic from the beginning and encourage them to take the children to the library to look for books about seagulls in particular, but other sea birds too, or to contribute any books from home.

- Ask parents and carers to encourage the children to keep a diary to record any sightings of seagulls in the fields round about. The record can be pictorial and/or have a written description, which the adults and children can create together.

- ➤ Seagulls will quite often flock to school playing fields, so binoculars should be at hand for the children to make their observations when the opportunity arises.

- ➤ Arrange a time to view the video clip (see Websites, page 48).

- ➤ Review the pictures taken at the beach with the digital camera (see page 7) and see if there are any with pictures of seagulls.

Activity content

1   Refer to the concept map of the sea (see page 3), and see if the children can identify any birds that live by the sea. They will probably have identified seagull and penguin. However, if your setting is situated very close to the seashore or if some of the children are keen birdwatchers, they might have a greater number of birds to offer. Ask the children to circle the birds as they are identified on the map.

2   Show the video clip of the seagull laying its eggs and sitting on its nest until the babies hatch out. Watch them feeding their young until they have grown feathers and are strong enough to fly and feed themselves.

3   Allow time for the children to share their own experiences. Some may have seen a nest on the cliff top, or on the roof of a neighbour's house. Very young children may have been frightened by large herring gulls swooping down and taking their food out of their hand, as these birds can become very bold if they are used to being fed. Encourage the children to share experiences of feeding other water birds, for example, feeding the ducks and swans in the local park. Talk with the children about the weed, frogs and fish that water birds like to eat.

4   Make your own trip to the local park and take some bread to encourage the birds to come close. If swans are present, they need watching, as they can be as bold as the seagulls and might frighten the children. However, you should attract a variety of ducks, geese, coots and moorhens and there are likely to be seagulls circling in the background for the children to see.

5   Use the digital camera to record as much of the scene as possible to make up into a book when you return to the classroom (see page 7).

6   Set up an observation site near to one of the windows that looks out over an open space. Construct it with large wooden or cardboard boxes with an old curtain across the top to make a real hideout. Provide several pairs of binoculars and paper and pens to record sightings of any water birds in particular.

7   Talk about the difference in sound between a duck quacking and a seagull screeching.

Extending learning

Key questions

Q   What was happening in the video? What did you see?

Q   Have you seen water birds flying outside? How do they fly? Can you show me?

Q   Can all birds fly? Why not? Can all birds swim? Why not?

Q   What is the same about a penguin and a seagull? What is different?

Q   What do water birds like to eat mostly?

Q   What sounds did the water birds make?

Q   What do the birds do if we are very noisy? Why is that?

Key vocabulary

egg	coot	weed
nest	goose	fish
seagull	penguin	flying
duck	feathers	swimming
swan	wings	screeching
moorhen	hatch	quacking

Follow-up activities

■ Songs and rhymes about seagulls, for example, 'The Seagull' by James K. Baxter or 'Ten White Seagulls', Anon. (see Singing games and poems, page 48). For the second poem, ten children can act out the rhyme:

>   Ten white seagulls, just see them fly.
>   Over the mountain, and up to the sky.
>   Ten white seagulls crying aloud.
>   Spread out their wings, and fly over a cloud.
>   Ten white seagulls on a bright day.
>   Pretty white seagulls, fly, fly away!

■ Compare a penguin and a seagull. Ask the children what is the same and what is different about these two birds. The children can make a large collage of a seagull and a penguin from pieces of torn black and white tissue paper, overlapping them to make grey where necessary. As the children identify the differences and similarities between the two, record them on a chart. For example, both are birds, live near to the sea, eat fish, are mostly black and white, but penguins cannot fly. Seagulls can fly and swim on the water, but penguins can swim under the water. The children might also identify the fact that, whereas seagulls have wings, penguins have flippers.

2 Story: *The Lighthouse Keeper's Lunch*

This activity is built round this charming story by Ronda and David Armitage that has become a modern children's classic. Every day, Mrs Grinling makes her husband a delicious lunch and sends it over on a special pulley to the lighthouse where he is the keeper. But on the way, the seagulls keep stealing his lunch. The Grinlings eventually come up with a successful plan to foil the seagulls.

⬣ Links to the Foundation Stage Curriculum

PD   Recognise the importance of keeping healthy, and the things which contribute to this.

CLL   Enjoy listening to and using spoken and written language, and readily turn to it in their play and learning.

Adult:child ratio 1:8

⬣ Resources

- ✔ Copy of *The Lighthouse Keeper's Lunch*, by Ronda and David Armitage (see Book bank, page 48)
- ✔ Video player, the nature video
- ✔ Fresh fruit: a pineapple, a banana, an apple, an orange, some cherries, a bunch of red grapes
- ✔ A picnic basket
- ✔ Food and drink as decided by the children (see page 41)
- ✔ String for the pulley and a wheel with a grooved rim

⬣ Preparation

- ➤ Acquire at least one copy of *The Lighthouse Keeper's Lunch* and arrange a time for the story session.
- ➤ Book the video player for a session to watch the nature clip again, especially the part where the seagulls begin to feed, swooping down to catch the fish.
- ➤ Gather together the other resources to make the props for the story.

Activity content

1 Visit the video clip or the webcam of a seagull feeding (see Websites, page 48).

2 Read the story to the children several times. If you have bilingual children, arrange to have a staff member who speaks their first language, or a parent or carer, to read the story too, or to follow up with questions.

3 Encourage the children to describe the setting for the story, what happened and who the main characters were.

4 Ask the children what the Grinlings did the first time to try to frighten the seagulls and why it had not worked.

5 Talk to the children about the successful solution. Ask the children why the seagulls did not like the mustard sandwiches, and where they went for their lunch after that. Give the children a tiny taste of the mustard if they have not tried it.

6 Look at the various items that Mrs Grinling made for her husband on the first day the lunch was stolen: 'A Mixed Seafood Salad, A Lighthouse Sandwich, Cold Chicken Garni, Sausages and Crisps, Peach Surprise, Iced Sea Biscuits, Drinks and Assorted Fruit'. Talk about the items in their lunch box. Discuss which items are healthy to eat every day and which should be kept for a special treat now and again.

7 Encourage the children to talk about their own experiences of the trip to the beach and to the park. Ask them if they saw the birds snatch anyone's food. Talk to them about what happened and what they think the person felt like. Ask them what they would do if the seagulls had stolen their lunch.

8 Encourage the children to talk about their own favourite foods and which fruits they have tasted.

Extending learning

Key questions

Q Who is the story about? What is happening? What does Mrs Grinling try first to scare the seagulls? Does it work? Why not?

Q Which plan is successful? Why does it work? Have you tasted mustard? What is it like? How can people use it in food?

Q What food did Mrs Grinling make for her husband's lunch on the first day it was stolen? Which part would you like to eat? Which food would be good/bad for Mr Grinling to eat every day? Why?

Q What did Mr Grinling feel like when his lunch was stolen?

Q How could we use a pulley in our room?

Q Which of these fruits in the picture do you like the best? Which is your favourite? Why do you like the taste? What shall we put in our fruit salad?

Q What shall we put in our picnic basket to take to the park?

Key vocabulary

Mr and Mrs Grinling
lighthouse
seagulls
lunch basket

pulley
Hamish the cat
mustard sandwiches

Follow-up activities

■ Buy the fruits recorded for Mr Grinling's lunch and with the children cut them up into small pieces for a snack time fruit salad. Save a few pieces of each for the children to try and find out which fruit is the most popular. Get the children to draw a picture of their favourite fruit and make a block graph with pictures to put on the wall. Be sure to talk afterwards about fruits that were not represented in the story. The children can then say which is their favourite fruit of all. They can send Mrs Grinling a message telling her to put their favourite fruit in the picnic basket for Mr Grinling.

■ Make up a picnic lunch to take to the park. Discuss with the children what should go in the basket and then involve the children in the preparation. They will need to decide how much food will be needed and how it will be eaten. For example, will it all be finger food or will eating utensils be necessary. They will need to decide on the best drink to take and whether it should be in small cartons or a big bottle poured into paper cups. After the children have finished, the leftover bread can be offered to the water birds.

■ Make a pulley with the children to carry items across the room. Talk about the uses of this and how the items will need to be packaged.

■ Have other stories and information books available about seagulls or other water birds (see Book bank, page 48).

3   A bird mobile

In this activity the children make some seagulls to add to the sea display. It is important that the birds be as individual as possible, and that the children be given the freedom to design their own birds within the constraints of using the three colours black, white and grey, to provide the continuity and to help distinguish the birds as seagulls. Support can be given in terms of the materials provided and in the talk that goes on around the activity.

⬡ **Links to the Foundation Stage Curriculum**

MD   Use shapes appropriately for tasks

CD   Begin to describe the texture of things

Adult:child ratio 1:6

⬡ **Resources**

- ✔ Pictures, paintings, photographs or posters showing seagulls
- ✔ Thick card of a neutral shade
- ✔ Black and white tissue paper
- ✔ Glue
- ✔ Stapler (used by the children with support)
- ✔ Hole puncher, hole reinforcements
- ✔ White, grey or black feathers (see Equipment, page 48)
- ✔ Felt-tip pens, pencils and crayons, small black and yellow felt-tip pens
- ✔ Large sheet of paper with large felt-tip pen

⬡ **Preparation**

- ➤ Add the pictures of seagulls to the sea display (see page 2).
- ➤ Gather all the disposable resources together and make them available in separate containers.
- ➤ Have some general shapes of seagulls in flight. Depending on the age and coordination skills of the children, these shapes may be needed for direct use, to be drawn round as templates, or simply used as examples of the approximate size and shape for the children to draw from. (These are only to be used as a standby, if the children are unable to create their own basic shape.)
- ➤ Tear up a source of white and black tissue paper piles to act as a starter; the children can continue to tear their own pieces after this.
- ➤ Provide some feathers for the children to add for decoration.
- ➤ Prepare the glue in suitable containers. Water-based glue will be sufficient for this delicate paper.
- ➤ Provide a hole puncher and the hole reinforcements.
- ➤ Have the stapler to hand if it is needed.

Activity content

1 First, look at the pictures of the seagulls with the children. This might require a walk over to the sea display or to the book corner.

2 Talk about the characteristics of seagulls: their size, their colours, the shape and colour of their bills.

3 Draw a picture of a seagull on the large sheet of paper as the children identify its various parts. Look carefully at the seagull's feet and talk about the fact that they are webbed and how this helps it to swim.

4 Encourage the children to draw and construct their birds as they wish, although based on the discussions you have had above. If some children do not know where to begin, then ask them about the parts of the bird that they have just identified. Ask what shape they want to choose for the body. Some very young children might need the additional support of the template designs (see page 42).

5 Make it clear to the children that the tissue paper can be torn again and made into any shape they want.

6 Talk about how to achieve a grey colour by overlapping the black and white tissue paper. Some of the children may have been involved in the construction of the large seagull and penguin and will have already experienced this technique.

7 Talk about the need to use the glue sparingly so that the paper does not become too wet.

8 The children will have to decorate both sides of their seagull; this will involve some matching exercises. Talk about whether you can see the individual feathers on a seagull when it is flying. There might be the need to add just one or two for effect. Talk about the smoothness of its bill and how this might be achieved perhaps by colouring it in with a felt-tip pen.

9 When a seagull is ready, a hole can be punched in the top of the body, and hole reinforcements added before it is hung from a wire mobile or a wire coat hanger and suspended over the sea display (see page 2).

Extending learning

Key questions

Q Can you tell me about this seagull? What is it like? What shape is its wing? Its bill? Does it look different from this one? How is it different? What things are the same?

Q Which shape will you choose for the body? What do we call that shape? Do you want to change it?

Q Which colour do you want now? What is it called? How will you make grey? Can you make it lighter or darker?

Q Where will you put the eyes? How will you do that?

Q Can you see the seagull's feathers when it is flying? What does its back look like?

Q Can you see its feet when it is flying? Where are they? How do its feet help when it is swimming? Can you draw the feet with the web between the toes?

Key vocabulary

bird	webbed foot	white
body	feathers	black
bill	circle	yellow
wing	oval	large
leg	grey	small

● Follow-up activities

■ Encourage the children to continue making their own seagulls using a variety of card, paper and feathers (see Equipment, page 48). If they make one with its mouth wide open, the children can stick it onto the outside of an empty cereal packet and cut out a hole behind the mouth. Small fish can then be drawn, cut out and fed to the seagull. This can become a more formalised game with children turning up a numbered card in turn and 'feeding' the appropriate number of fish to the gull.

■ Mount the pictures taken of the children at the park onto stiff card and talk to the children about what the caption should say. Write the words under the picture and laminate each one. Design and laminate a cover with the children, perhaps using a picture of the children on the park visit (see page 36). When all the pages have been laminated, punch two holes in the left side of each one and strengthen them with clear plastic hole reinforcements. Finally, assemble the book using a loose leafed ring binder. Alternatively, staple the pages together. Put the book on the display table so the children have constant access to it.

■ Related stories, rhymes and poems can be accessed from the Book bank (see page 48 for suggested titles).

Encourage independent learning

Water

Additional resources

- ✔ Salt-water tray
- ✔ Water plants (seaweed if possible)
- ✔ Fishing boats
- ✔ Large and small stones

- ✔ Rubber fish
- ✔ Lighthouse
- ✔ Model seagulls

Possible activities/learning outcomes

KUW Comment and ask questions about where they live and the natural world.

Create a bay in the water tray by filling it with salt water and fastening water plants/seaweed on the bottom with heavy stones.

Use large stones and gravel or pebbles on the bottom and put in small model fish and seagulls (see Equipment, page 48).

On one large flat stone stand a lighthouse; this could be a large plastic cone.

Encourage the children to act out the story of *Louis the Lifeboat: The Nasty Black Stuff* by Gordon Volke (see Book bank, page 48). Louis rescues a seagull who is covered in oil from a tanker spillage. The story features the lifeboat, a seagull, a lighthouse and an oil tanker. Pieces of black bin liner could be used to simulate the oil slick and be wrapped around the seagull (see page 4).

Create narratives and rhymes based on a bird's life by the sea.

The practitioner role

▲ Talk to the children about the birds that cannot fly (use 'Why Can't I Fly? see Book bank, page 48) and then see if they can identify those that can walk, fly and swim.

▲ Ducks, geese and swans will fall in to this category as well as the seagulls and there are many stories to read and tell about these birds (see Book bank, page 48).

▲ Retell the rhyme about the 'Ten White Seagulls' with the children and encourage them to act it out in the water.

▲ Encourage the children to think about when seagulls might need to walk, when they might need to swim and when they might need to fly.

▲ Support the children by asking open-ended questions about the environment of the seashore and how this compares to their own homes.

▲ Talk about the disaster of an oil spillage and what that means for all the wildlife along the coast.

Malleable materials

Additional resources

- ✔ 450g self-raising flour
- ✔ 300g margarine
- ✔ 200g sugar
- ✔ 2 eggs
- ✔ Oven
- ✔ Baking tray
- ✔ Mixing bowl

- ✔ Wooden spoon
- ✔ Rolling pins
- ✔ Board
- ✔ Biscuit cutters in the shape of a shell, a boat and a bird
- ✔ Sieve
- ✔ Cooling rack

Possible activities/learning outcomes

KUW Use simple tools and techniques competently and appropriately.

Make 60 'sea' biscuits, as Mrs Grinling does in the story. The children can be involved in the purchase of the ingredients, share in the mixing and all have the opportunity to roll out and create their own individual biscuits.

Pre-heat the oven to 180°C/350°F/Gas mark 4.

Sift the flour into a bowl.

Rub in margarine finely.

Add the sugar.

Mix with the spoon to a very stiff dough with the beaten eggs.

Wrap the dough in aluminium foil or a plastic bag and put in the fridge for 30 minutes.

Then give each child some dough to roll out.

Use biscuit cutters to create the shape of a shell, a boat or a bird (in the story a pattern is made with icing, but this will be difficult for young children to manage).

Place the biscuits on the greased baking tray and bake for 12 to 15 minutes.

Leave on the trays for 2 to 3 minutes before transferring the biscuits to a cooling rack prior to distribution at snack time, or on a picnic in the park.

The practitioner role

- ▲ Encourage the children to recall the story of *The Lighthouse Keeper's Lunch*.
- ▲ Support the children in collating a list of items needed to make the sea biscuits.
- ▲ Introduce and encourage the children to use the vocabulary of manipulation, such as *sieve, mix, squeeze, bend, smooth out, shape, roll*.
- ▲ Support the children's mathematical language by encouraging them to count the number of biscuits on each tray.
- ▲ As an alternative another day you could suggest making 'Lighthouse Sandwiches'. The children could suggest the ingredients, and be involved in the purchase of the ingredients, the preparation, assembly and distribution of the sandwiches for snack time.

Role play

Additional resources

- ✔ Lighthouse
- ✔ Kitchen
- ✔ Pulley
- ✔ Basket
- ✔ Some model or real food

- ✔ Seagulls
- ✔ Hamish the cat
- ✔ Seagull masks: thin card, staples, hole puncher and hole reinforcements, shirring elastic

---

Possible activities/learning outcomes

PD Create equipment by means of pushing and pulling movements.

The children act out the story of *The Lighthouse Keeper's Lunch*.

Having been involved in making a large-scale pulley in the setting, they will enjoy making their own version and gathering together items for the lunch, which could include plastic fruit and cakes.

Additional items can be made with dough.

Mr and Mrs Grinling will need to be positioned in the lighthouse and the kitchen respectively with the pulley set up between them. Some of the children can become the seagulls flying down and stealing the lunch.

A toy cat can be sent out in the basket.

The practitioner role

▲ Talk about the characters needed in the story and what they felt like at different times.

▲ If the seagulls wish to dress up, assist in the preparation of some masks that can be held on with shirring elastic around the head (see Photocopiable sheet 3).

▲ Stimulate the children's imagination by re-reading *The Lighthouse Keeper's Lunch* and telling other stories and rhymes about seagulls and other seabirds to enable them to gain confidence in constructing their own narratives.

Book bank

Information books

Birds (Baby Einstein Board Book) by Julie Aigner-Clark (2002). Scholastic Children's Books. ISBN 043997321X

The Burgess Bird Book for Children by Thornton W. Burgess (2003). Indypublish.com. ISBN 1404362452

Feathers, Flippers and Feet by Deborah Lock (2004). Dorling Kindersley. ISBN 075136794X

Seagulls at the Seashore (2003) by Maxim. Dorrance Publishing. ISBN 0805955216

I Eat Fruit! (Things I Eat) by Hannah Tofts and Rupert Horrox (2001). Zero to Ten. ISBN 1840891629. This book has flaps which when lifted reveal the pips, stones and seeds inside the various fruits.

Websites

Amazon: www.amazon.co.uk (*Bird* video from the Dorling Kindersley Eyewitness Series)

Baker Ross: www.bakerross.co.uk

BBC: www.bbc.co.uk/nature/animals/birds/webcams

BBC: www.bbc.co.uk/northernireland/education

Disney Educational Productions: http://dep.disney.go.com/educational (*Birds* video) (26 minutes)

Early Learning Centre: www.elc.co.uk

Early Literature: www.earlyliterature.ecsd.net/birds%20general.htm

Learning Resources: www.learningresources.com

Library Video: www.libraryvideo.com (*Birds and Rodents*) (30 minutes)

Story books

The Lighthouse Keeper's Lunch by Ronda and David Armitage (1994). Scholastic. ISBN 0590551752. Seagulls, lighthouse.

Seymour's Night Flight: The Adventures of a Nantucket Seagull by Heather Barlow Sheldon (2004). Cassiopeia Press. ISBN 0976182009

Why Can't I Fly? by Ken Brown (2001). Ipicturebooks. ISBN 1590194241

Kipper's Beach Ball by Mick Inkpen (2004). Hodder Children's Books. ISBN 0340879017. The ball makes the seagulls squawk, knocks the top off a sandcastle into the surf and rides on a great breaking wave (a giant wave).

Fergus the Sea Dog by Tony Maddox (2004). Piccadilly Press. ISBN 1953407194

Billy and the Seagulls by Paul May (2004). Corgi. ISBN 0552551589. Billy is scared of everything, including the seagulls when they move to the seaside. The story explores whether his brother, Eddie, and his stepfather can find ways to help Billy get over his fears.

Sglod at Sea (Pont Hoppers) by Ruth Morgan and illustrated by Suzanne Carpenter (2001). Pont. ISBN 185902937X

Curious George Goes to the Beach by H.A. Rey (1999). Houghton Mifflin. ISBN 0395978343

Zeynep: The Seagull of Galata Tower by Julia Townend (2003). Citlembik Publications. ISBN 9756663324. Set in Istanbul.

Louis the Lifeboat: The Nasty Black Stuff by Gordon Volke, illustrated Colin Bowler (2002). Ravette Publishing. ISBN 1841611190

The Seagull Who Was Afraid to Fly by Steven P. Wickstrom (2004). PublishAmerica. ISBN 1413718906 (older children)

Singing games and poems

'Seagull, Seagull Sit on the Shore' by Anon. in *This Little Puffin: A Treasury of Nursery Rhymes, Songs and Games* compiled by Elizabeth Matterson (1991). Puffin Books. ISBN 0140340483

'Ten White Seagulls' by Anon. www.earlyliterature.ecsd.net/birds%20general.htm (accessed 15/08/2005)

'The Seagull' by James K. Baxter. www.bookcouncil.org.nz/community/media/baxterposter.pdf (accessed 15/08/2005)

Seaside Poems edited by Jill Bennett and illustrated by Nick Sharratt (1998). Oxford University Press. ISBN 0192761749

Equipment

Collage Feathers and Sequins. www.bakerross.co.uk Tel: 0870 241 1867

Lightweight Binoculars. Magnification to the factor of six. www.elc.co.uk Tel: 08705 352 352 (3yrs +)

Mini Beasts. www.elc.co.uk Tel: 08705 352 352 (3yrs +)

Play Food Bumper Pack. www.elc.co.uk Tel: 08705 352 352 (3yrs +)

Fruit and Vegetable Play Food Baskets. www.learningresources.com Tel: 01553 762276 (3yrs +)

4

Ship

Links to the Foundation Stage Curriculum

Follow-up Activities

Home–setting Links

Ship

Extending Learning

Resources and Preparation

Activity Content

Adult-led focus activities

1 Observation

There will be very few children living in the United Kingdom who have never seen a boat or ship of some kind, even if it is only a paddle boat in the local park. Those whose settings are in coastal areas, near ports or near harbours will have heard and seen ocean-going liners, ferries, cargo boats and sailing yachts on a regular basis. Those who live near lakes, canals or rivers, too, will have had the opportunity to see motorboats and narrowboats. Some will have been to the seaside on holiday and others will have travelled to the Isle of Wight, the Channel Islands, France or Ireland on a ferry. For others, ships will mean working vessels, such as fishing boats leaving late at night and returning in the early morning with their catch.

⬢ Links to the Foundation Stage Curriculum

CLL   Question why things happen and give explanations.

KUW   Investigate objects and materials by using all of their senses as appropriate.

Adult:child ratio 1:2 for a trip to a harbour, a river/canal ride or a boating lake

⬢ Resources

✔ Boating venue to visit

✔ Copy of *Ferryboat Ride!* by Anne Rockwell, other story and information books about ships (see Book bank, page 60)

✔ Model and toy ships

✔ Digital camera and/or a video camera

✔ Paper and pencils (for recording purposes)

✔ Large sheet of paper with a felt-tip pen

✔ Lightweight binoculars

✔ Passport

Preparation

➤ If your setting is within an appropriate distance from a harbour, a river/canal or a boating lake, make a preparatory visit to inspect the facilities and to find out if there are any appropriate activities already provided for the age group of your children, and if not, decide on some activities of your own devising.

➤ Arrange a date for a visit and make the booking with the venue, if necessary, and your transport providers. Decide if you are going to take the children for a ride or just to view the ships and boats.

Home–setting links

● Write letters to the parents and carers about the trip to make it clear what is happening and what is needed in terms of funds, food and offers of support on the trip.

● Let the parents and carers know about the ship topic from the beginning and encourage them to take the children to the library to look for story and information books about ships and boats.

● Ask parents and carers to encourage the children to keep a diary to record sightings of water transport and to recall any trips the family might have already made. The record can be pictorial and/or have a written description, which the adults and children can create together.

● Ask the parents and carers if they have any model ships and boats that they would be willing to lend for display purposes.

➤ Put together a book box of story, poetry and information books about ships and harbours, lakes, rivers and canals (see Book bank, pages 60–61).

➤ Gather together the resources listed above.

Activity content

1   Refer to the concept map of the sea (see page 3) and see if the children can identify transport that is useful for travelling on the sea. They might identify items such as a ship, a boat, a ferry, a hovercraft, a catamaran, a yacht, a motorboat; encourage them to circle these on the concept map.

2   Ask the children about their experiences of travelling in a ship and talk about the reasons for their trip. Encourage them to describe what the ship/boat was like inside, the process from entering the vessel to leaving the harbour at the other end and the feelings the trip generated.

3   Raise the question of when a passport is needed. Share your own experiences of sea travel and examine your passport with the children; some children may bring in their own passports to share.

4   Read *Ferryboat Ride!* to the children (see Book bank, page 60). This story uses rich language and the children will be able to imagine themselves alongside the little girl as she watches the water, feeds the gulls, peers through the fog and hears the foghorn blasts. Although the correct terminology is used throughout, it is done in such a natural way that it should help the children's understanding.

5   Talk about the different parts of a ship. As the children mention a part, draw it on a large piece of paper until all the parts are assembled. Talk about why each part is important.

6 Make your visit to the chosen venue, drawing on the expertise of any staff or using your own prepared materials.

7 Use the digital camera to take photographs of the children: their embarkation, on board, the engine room (if appropriate), having lunch, views across the water.

8 Have the binoculars available for the children to use to observe birds and other boats from the ship or from the harbour wall.

9 Use the printed photographs for the sea display (see page 2).

10 Display any model ships and boats purchased or loaned.

11 Talk to the children about boats with engines, those with sails driven by the wind, those with oars, those pushed along with poles.

12 Talk about the different uses for ships and boats and make a list with the children.

Extending learning

Key questions

Q Has anyone been on a ship or a boat? How did you get to the port? Can you tell us what you remember? What did you have to do first?

Q What did it feel like when you set sail? What did you do on the ship?

Q What did it feel like when you walked around? Did your legs feel wobbly?

Q What was it like when you landed? Did it take a long time for everyone to get off?

Q Can anyone tell us the name of any part of a ship? Do you know what it does?

Q Did you need to have a passport for your trip? What was it like? Can you show us? Why did you need one? Why not?

Q What can you see through your binoculars?

Q How do ships and boats move? Can you think of any different ways?

Q What are ships and boats used for? How many things can you think of?

Key vocabulary		
ship	car deck	sail
engine	restaurant	wind
deck	gangplank	oar
funnel	yacht	pole

Follow-up activities

■ Act out the poem 'The Ferryman' by Christina Rossetti (see Book bank, page 61) with the children. Wooden blocks can be stood up on their edges on the floor in the shape of a rowing boat with two rows of blocks set across, flat side up, to act as seats. Flat pieces of wood can be used as oars or you may have plastic ones available. The children can take it in turns to row or to be the passenger. All the children can be involved in saying the rhyme, with one half being the voice of the passenger and the other half the ferryman.

- Other songs and rhymes can be shared with the same equipment, such as 'Row, Row, Row Your Boat' (see Singing games and poems, page 61). Talk to the children about where rivers come from and how they all run out to the sea.

- Very young children can share a board book, which gives accurate details of a ship (see Book bank, page 60).

- Select some of the photographs taken on the trip; mount and laminate them to make into books (see pages 44 or 81) or jigsaw puzzles (see page 87) for the children. They will particularly enjoy the ones in which they feature.

2　Story: *The Best Place on Earth*

This activity is built round the story of *The Best Place on Earth* by Becky Bloom (see Book bank, page 60). Miss Hedgehog's aunt invites her to visit the Mediterranean island where she lives. Miss Hedgehog decides to ask her woodland friends to join her and they are all very pleased except for young Beaver, who has never left the forest before. For him, home is the best place on earth, but after swimming in the sea, playing on the beach, hiking on the cliffs and tasting all the wonderful new meals, he does not want to leave the island when it is time to return.

 Links to the Foundation Stage Curriculum

PSE　Consider the consequences of their words and actions for themselves and others.

CLL　Sustain attentive listening, responding to what they have heard by relevant comments, questions or actions.

Adult:child ratio 1:6

Resources

- ✔ Copy of *The Best Place on Earth* by Becky Bloom (see Book bank, page 60)
- ✔ Eduzone native animal finger puppets (see Equipment, page 61)
- ✔ Felt-tip pens
- ✔ Scissors
- ✔ Sticky labels
- ✔ Old cardboard box, empty cardboard container
- ✔ Empty plastic bottles
- ✔ Big old key (this can be made out of cardboard and covered with aluminium foil)

Preparation

➤ Acquire a copy of *The Best Place on Earth* and arrange a time for the story session.

➤ Purchase animal finger puppets, or provide the materials to make them with the children.

➤ Gather together the resources listed above and be ready to add others that the children identify.

Home–setting link

Arrange for parents or carers to tell the story in other languages if appropriate.

Activity content

1 Read the story to the children several times. If you have bilingual children, arrange to have a staff member who speaks their first language, or a parent or carer, to read the story too, or to follow up with questions.

2 Encourage the children to describe the setting for the story, what happened and who the main characters are.

3 Talk about the fears that young Beaver has. Ask the children if they have ever been afraid of going to a strange place. Encourage them to share what their fears were and whether things turned out to be as bad as they expected them to be. Some children may be able to relate this experience to starting school. For example, they might identify leaving their mum, eating different food, using the same toilet as everyone else, fear of big boys and girls, fear of being expected to do hard sums, not having any friends, not being able to understand what the teacher says (this might be because the teacher speaks a different language, has a different accent, or because the child has a hearing impairment).

4 Reflect on the story and talk about all the different activities the friends enjoyed.

5 Encourage the children to talk about the things that they do with their friends. Talk with them about what makes a good friend.

6 The animals made a beautiful boat from an old crate, some plastic bottles, an old key and an empty can. Let the children try to make their own boat with these items. For safety reasons use a cardboard container rather than an aluminium tin, which might have a sharp edge.

7 Involve the children in making simple finger puppets by dividing an address label into four and drawing one of the characters on each quarter. The children can then peel off the picture labels and stick the characters onto their fingertips. These puppets will only last for one play session, but can easily be replaced and new characters added as the children develop their own stories.

8 Alternatively, use the purchased animal puppets to act out the different parts of the story. In the Eduzone pack there is a rabbit, a hedgehog and a badger. There is no mouse, but a simple cone of paper slipped onto a finger with eyes, ears and whiskers drawn in can make a simple substitute.

9 Decide on one aspect of the story to retell using the puppets.

● Extending learning

Key questions

Q What is young Beaver afraid of?

Q In the story, what was it like on the ferry? Have you ever felt seasick?

Q What was it like on the beach?

Q What activities did the friends enjoy? What do you like to do on the beach?

Q Why did they use sun lotion? How can you keep safe on the beach? What could be dangerous?

Q What did the animals use to build their beautiful boat? Can you make one too?

Key vocabulary		
hedgehog	ferry	fishing
rabbit	seasick	crate
badger	sun lotion	key
mouse	water	bottles
aunt	beach	empty can
beaver	snorkelling	

● Follow-up activities

- Encourage the children to act out various events in the story and to begin to develop some storylines of their own.

- Make model boats from the round lid of a margarine tub. A right-angled triangle is cut out of thin card and decorated for the sail. Holes are punched at intervals along the straight edge of the sail and a straw is threaded through the holes and attached to the lid by a piece of play dough or Plasticine shaped like a boat. Alternatively, a cocktail stick can be taped to the sail instead of using the straw. If the lid is painted blue, then this will look like the sea. Flags can be added if desired.

3 Make your own port

The water tray indoors or the paddling pool outdoors will be central to this activity and provide the children with the opportunity to establish some lively play with ships and boats coming in and out of the port to load and unload their cargo. Large wooden or plastic blocks can be built up as the docks right up to the water with warehouses and offices built with other construction materials such as Lego. Large cranes can be made available (see Equipment, page 61) to move the cargo on and off the ships. Lifeboats can be available for sea rescue with the coastguard positioned centrally to coordinate events.

● Links to the Foundation Stage Curriculum

PD Manipulate materials and objects by picking up, releasing, arranging, threading and posting them.

CD Play alongside other children who are engaged in the same theme.

Adult:child ratio 1:4

Resources

- ✔ Large wooden boxes and blocks
- ✔ Plastic boxes and small cubes
- ✔ Cranes (see Equipment, page 61)
- ✔ Lego and other construction materials
- ✔ Goggles, flippers
- ✔ Model ships and boats (see Equipment, page 61)
- ✔ Trucks
- ✔ Lifebelts
- ✔ Pulleys

Preparation

➤ Decide whether the port is to be positioned indoors or outdoors. If you have a purpose-built paddling pool, then this would be the obvious venue. If mobile pools are to be used or large water trays, then consideration needs to be given to their position. Play will be enhanced if the children can actually walk around in the water.

➤ Gather together the above materials and be ready to provide other items as the children's play develops.

Activity content

1 Read some of the stories and rhymes from the Book bank (see pages 60–62). For example, *Who Sank the Boat?* by Pamela Allen, and Christina Rossetti's poem, 'Storm-wind'. These will provide the inspiration for the children's play.

2 Talk to the children about the docks and what you might use to build them, and the smaller warehouses and office buildings.

3 Talk about how the cargo will be moved. The children may remember setting up pulleys from previous sessions. There may be trucks lined up by the water to carry the products to the shops and markets, and cranes available.

4 Allow the children great freedom in playing with the ships and boats and developing their own narratives.

5 Many model ships and boats should be available, including lifeboats. Some children might decide to have helicopters present for air-sea rescue, (see Equipment, page 61).

6 Talk about safety issues, radio weather forecasts, coastguard warnings of changing conditions. Lifebelts and divers should be ready to make underwater searches; snorkelling gear can be provided with flippers and goggles.

7 Although adult directives should be light, adult supervision will be vital because of the danger of young children drowning in even very shallow water (see page 4).

Extending learning

Key questions

Q What could you use to build the docks? Where will you put them? Can all the ships come up to the dockside? Why not?

Q How will the cargo be carried on and off the ships and boats? Where will the goods be stored? How will the food get to the shops and the markets?

Q What do ships' captains need to know about the weather? How can they find out about that?

Q Who will help if a ship is in danger? Which rescue services will be needed?

Q If you are in a boat, what should you always wear to be safe?

Key vocabulary

ships	docks	weather report
boats	port	coastguard
engines	cargo	life jackets
sails	transport	

Follow-up activities

- Encourage the children to look at various items and predict whether they will float or sink. They can test out their theory and put the items in a labelled container.

- Experiments can be carried out using model boats to see how much cargo each one can hold before it sinks. The children can use small wooden cubes as the cargo and count them to see which boat can hold the most weight.

Encourage independent learning

Water

Additional resources

- ✔ Water tray
- ✔ Small model boats including pirate ships (see Equipment, page 61)
- ✔ Toy rescue helicopters (see Equipment, page 61)
- ✔ Balsa wood or sticks
- ✔ Thin string
- ✔ Walnut shells
- ✔ Cocktail sticks
- ✔ Plasticine

Possible activities/learning outcomes

CLL Begin to make patterns in their experience through linking cause and effect, sequencing, ordering and grouping.

Place small boats made from different materials in a water tray for the children to sail and to test their buoyancy and their capacity to carry cargo.

Use helicopters and boats for the children to act out a rescue situation as part of their play.

The practitioner role

▲ Encourage the children to use walnut shells as small boats, and to lash wooden sticks together to make rafts to sail alongside larger boats.

▲ When testing the buoyancy, help the children to predict which ones will float for the longest distance and which will carry the most weight and to explain the processes involved; record the outcomes they have observed.

▲ Gather the resources together and be prepared to find additional materials as the children's play develops.

▲ Encourage the children to draw on their own experiences, as well as those they have encountered in stories, as they engage in developing their own narratives.

Creative area

Additional resources

- ✔ Tape recorder, a tape on which practitioners have recorded songs and rhymes, or a commercially produced tape including these rhymes (see Singing games and poems, page 61)

Possible activities/learning outcomes

PD Go backwards and sideways as well as forwards.

CD Enjoy joining in with dancing and ring games.

Introduce a ring game such as:

> The big ship sails through the Alley, Alley O;
> Alley, Alley O; Alley, Alley O,
> The big ship sails on the Alley, Alley O
> On the last day of September.
> The captain said, 'It will never, never do;
> Never, never do; never, never, do' . . .
> The big ship sank to the bottom of the sea;
> The bottom of the sea; the bottom of the sea . . .
> We all dip our heads in the deep blue sea;
> The deep blue sea; the deep blue sea . . .

(See Singing games and poems, page 61.)

The children hold hands in a line and the child at one end puts an arm up against the wall to form an arch. The child at the other end of the line then goes through the arch and the others follow. At the end, the child touching the wall is twisted round so that his arms are crossed. This child and the one next to him or her then raise their arms to form an arch for the children to go through. During this process the first verse is sung repeatedly and continues until all the children have crossed arms. The children then form a circle holding hands, but still with their arms crossed. They then continue through the other verses displaying appropriate actions to accompany the words.

Teach the children other poems about creatures who went to sea in a variety of vessels. For example:

- 'The Jumblies' (by Edward Lear), who went to sea in a sieve;
- 'The Owl and the Pussy-Cat' (by Edward Lear), who went to sea in a beautiful pea-green boat.

(See Singing games and poems, page 61.)

The practitioner role

▲ Encourage the children to move both individually and as part of a group.

▲ Help them to understand and respond to directional instructions as they join in the action rhymes.

▲ Teach the children the traditional words and actions of the songs and rhymes and then encourage them to play these independently and to develop their own versions.

▲ Talk with the children about which materials make a successful boat, especially in the light of the jumblies going to sea in a sieve.

▲ Provide the resources necessary to support these activities, and be ready to talk through suggestions for any new words and actions.

Book bank

Information books

Boat by B. Blathwayt (2000). Hutchinson Children's Books. ISBN 0091768470. Exploring a ferry ride.

Things That Go edited by Nicola Deschamps (2002). Dorling Kindersley. ISBN 0751339555. Board book with flaps.

The Little Book of Sand and Water by Sally Featherstone and illustrated by Rebecca Savania (2002). Featherstone Education. ISBN 1904187528

Rescue Vehicles by Jo Litchfield (2003). Usborne Publishing. ISBN 0746056834. Board book.

Seaplane (Go Books) by Meg Parsont and Anna Curti (1999). Abbeville Press. ISBN 0789205467. Board book.

Ships and Boats: Eye Openers by Angela Royston, Jane Cradock-Watson and Dave Hopkins (1992). Atheneum Books for Young Readers. ISBN 0689715668

Boats and Ships (Inside and Out) by Angela Royston and John Downs (1997). Rigby Interactive Library. ISBN 1575721708

Websites

Baker Ross: www.bakerross.co.uk

BIG Spielwarenfabrick: www.big.de

DKL Marketing: www.dkl.co.uk

Early Learning Centre: www.elc.co.uk

Eduzone: www.eduzone.co.uk

FEVA (UK): www.feva.co.uk

Playmobil UK: www.playmobil.com

Scottish songs and poems: www.rampantscotland.com

Wader Quality Toys UK: www.wadertoys.de

Story books

Who Sank the Boat? (Picture Puffin) by Pamela Allen (2000). Puffin. ISBN 0140566937

Tim and Lucy Go to Sea by Edward Ardizzone (1999). Scholastic Press. ISBN 0439010454

Where the Forest Meets the Sea by Jeannie Baker (1998). Walker Books. ISBN 0744563011

Olive's Pirate Party by Roberta Baker and illustrated by Debbie Tilley (2005). Little, Brown. ISBN 0316167924

An Island in the Sun by Stella Blackstone and Nicoletta Ceccoli (2002). Barefoot Books. ISBN 1841481920 (Foundation Stage, Key Stage 1)

Bella Goes to Sea by Benedict Blathwayt (1996). Red Fox. ISBN 0099681919

The Best Place on Earth by Becky Bloom (1999). Siphano Picture Books. ISBN 9607930266

Little Bear's Little Boat by Eve Bunting and illustrated by Nancy Carpenter (2004). Bloomsbury Publishing. ISBN 0747574782

Hushabye by John Burningham (2001). Knopf Books. ISBN 0375814140

Ships and Boats (All Aboard Series) by Peter Curry (2001). Picture Lions. ISBN 000136166X (0–2yrs)

Mr Little's Noisy Boat by Richard Fowler (1995). Mammoth. ISBN 0749710276

Pip Pirate (Fun Phones Series) (2004). Campbell Books. ISBN 140504070X. Board book shaped like a mobile phone; key terms: *ship, treasure, fisherman, walk the plank, crow's nest.*

The Shore Beyond by Mary Joslin and illustrated by Alison Jay (2001). Lion Publishing. ISBN 0745944639

Pirate Pete by Kim Kennedy and illustrated by Doug Kennedy (2002). Harry N. Abrams. ISBN 0810943565

I Saw a Ship a-Sailing by Sian Lewis and illustrated by Graham Howells (2001). Pont. ISBN 1859029086

Fergus the Sea Dog by Tony Maddox (2004). Piccadilly Press. ISBN 1953407194. Key words: *boat, storm, crab, seals, rock pools, weeds, seagulls, stores, fish.*

Lottie's New Beach Towel by Petra Mathers (illustrator) (2001). Aladdin. ISBN 0689844417

Sglod at Sea (Pont Hoppers) by Ruth Morgan and illustrated by Suzanne Carpenter (2001). Pont. ISBN 185902937X

Ferryboat Ride! by Anne Rockwell (1999). Knopf Books for Young Readers. ISBN 0517709597

Sailing Boat (Slide-Along-the-Slot-Books) by Helen Stephens (2003). Macmillan Children's Books. ISBN 0333968271

Singing games and poems

'The Big Ship Sails Through the Alley, Alley O' by Anon. in *This Little Puffin: A Treasury of Nursery Rhymes, Songs and Games* compiled by Elizabeth Matterson (1991). Puffin Books. ISBN 0140340483

'Row, Row, Row Your Boat' by Anon. in *This Little Puffin: A Treasury of Nursery Rhymes, Songs and Games* compiled by Elizabeth Matterson (1991). Puffin Books. ISBN 0140340483

'The Skye Boat Song' by Anon. www.rampantscotland.com/songs/blsongs_skye.htm (accessed 15/08/2005) Chorus:

> Speed bonnie boat like a bird on the wing
> Onward the sailors cry
> Carry the lad that's born to be king
> Over the sea to Skye

Seaside Poems edited by Jill Bennett and illustrated by Nick Sharratt (1998). Oxford University Press. ISBN 0192761749

'The Jumblies' by Edward Lear in *A Puffin Book of Verse* compiled by Eleanor Graham (1953). Penguin Books. ISBN 0140300724

'The Owl and the Pussy Cat' by Edward Lear in *A Puffin Book of Verse* compiled by Eleanor Graham (1953). Penguin Books. ISBN 0140300724

'The Voyage' by Joan Prince in *Happy Landings: Poems for the Youngest* (Zebra Books) edited by Howard Sergeant (1971). Evans Bros. ISBN 0237351897

'The Ferryman' by Christina Rossetti in *Happy Landings: Poems for the Youngest* (Zebra Books) edited by Howard Sergeant (1971). Evans Bros. ISBN 0237351897

'Storm-wind' by Christina Rossetti in *Happy Landings: Poems for the Youngest* (Zebra Books) edited by Howard Sergeant (1971). Evans Bros. ISBN 0237351897

Equipment

Acrylic Jewels. A sparkling assortment of shiny-backed coloured jewels. Sizes 7mm–23mm. Sold in packs of 100 or 300. www.bakerross.co.uk Tel: 0870 241 1867

Big Diggi Sandy. Designed to fit into a sandpit. Dredging shovel easy to use and can move a lot of sand. www.big.de Tel: 01296 662992 (3yrs +)

Big Jeff Bagger. This operational crane is designed to grab and lift and then to transport goods. www.big.de Tel: 01296 662992 (3yrs +)

Pirates Treasure. A wooden three-dimensional pirate ship with treasure that children can lock together. www.dkl.co.uk Tel: 01604 678780 (2yrs +)

Native Animal Puppets. www.eduzone.co.uk Tel: 08456 445 556

Collage Set of Coloured Match Sticks. www.elc.co.uk Tel: 08705 352 352 (3yrs +)

Collage Set of Mirrors and Beads. www.elc.co.uk Tel: 08705 352 352 (3yrs +)

Helicopter. www.elc.co.uk. Tel: 08705 352 352 (3yrs +)

Lightweight Binoculars. Magnification to the factor of six. www.elc.co.uk Tel: 08705 352 352 (3yrs +)

Pirate & Raft. Rolls on wheels. www.elc.co.uk Tel: 08705 352 352 (3yrs +)

Pirate & Row Boat. www.elc.co.uk Tel: 08705 352 352 (3yrs +)

Pirate Ship. With five characters, wheels, treasure chest and anchor. H38cm x W36cm. www.elc.co.uk Tel: 08705 352 352 (18mths +)

Transport 3-in-a-Box. Make a car, a train and a boat. Three 12-piece jigsaws in a box. www.elc.co.uk Tel: 08705 352 352 (2yrs +)

Wooden Pirate Ship. With cannons, crow's nest, plank, helm, anchor and sail. Runs on wheels. Additional Pirate Sticker Set, Cannons, Pirate's Accessories Set and four-piece Pirate Outfit. www.elc.co.uk Tel: 08705 352 352 (3yrs +)

Glitter Gems. A jewellery box with a range of gems and glitter for making jewellery as well as paints and glue for decorating the box. www.feva.co.uk Tel: 01494 460900 (6–10yrs)

Viking Longboat. A versatile toy that children can construct themselves with the crew and the rigging provided. www.playmobil.com Tel: 01268 490184 (4yrs +)

Baby Trucks. Can tip back and steer. www.wadertoys.de Tel: 01582 713943 (2yrs +)

5

Shark

Links to the Foundation Stage Curriculum

Follow-up Activities

Home–setting Links

Shark

Extending Learning

Resources and Preparation

Activity Content

Adult-led focus activities

1 Observation

The sea is full of fish of all colours, shapes and sizes and the largest of all are the sharks. Children will be fascinated by the mysterious world under the sea, in awe of its beauty and fearful of its strangeness. In the surface layer of the ocean, creatures like squid, basking sharks and seahorses feed on tiny plants and animals called plankton. In the middle layer of the ocean the fish feed on other fish. Some examples of these are the oarfish, which is long and thin; sometimes five times longer than a person. Its top fin looks like a ribbon and it has no tail. Hatchetfish on the other hand are shorter than an adult's hand and very flat. The giant squid has long tentacles, which it uses to catch other fish and the great white shark can grow as long as ten metres and is a very fierce fighter. On the bottom of the ocean some small fish have huge jaws, like the viperfish and gulper eel. The tripod fish has long fins, which let it rest on the seabed without sinking in. The children will enjoy discovering the variety of fish, especially if they have the opportunity to watch them swim.

⬢ **Links to the Foundation Stage Curriculum**

KUW Show an interest in the world in which they live.

CD Further explore an experience using a range of senses.

**Adult:child ratio
1:2 for a Sea Life Centre
or an aquarium visit;
1:8 for a video clip**

⬢ **Resources**

- ✔ A Sea Life Centre or an aquarium to visit
- ✔ Pictures of sharks and other fish
- ✔ Stories and information books and videos about fish (see Book bank, pages 74–75)
- ✔ Model and toy fish (see Equipment, page 75)
- ✔ Magnifying glasses
- ✔ Large sheet of paper with a felt-tip pen
- ✔ Digital camera and/or video camera
- ✔ Paper and writing utensils
- ✔ Paper plates
- ✔ Green pipe cleaners
- ✔ Tissue paper and glue

Preparation

➤ If your setting is within an appropriate distance from a Sea Life Centre (see Websites, page 74) or an aquarium (often available in garden centres), make a preparatory visit to inspect the facilities and to find out if there are any appropriate activities already provided for the age group of your children, and if not, decide on some activities of your own devising.

➤ Collect a number of video and film clips involving sharks and other fish to show to the children, for example, the Nemo stories (see Book bank, page 74). Video clips from nature programmes, such as those broadcast by David Attenborough for the BBC with hidden cameras, can show the life cycles of various fish including sharks at various stages of development (see Websites, page 74).

➤ Collect pictures and posters of sharks and other fish (see Websites, page 74).

➤ Arrange a date for the Sea Life Centre or aquarium visit and make the booking with the organisation concerned and with your transport providers.

Home–setting links

● Write letters to the parents and carers about the trip to make it clear what is happening and what is needed in terms of funds, food and offers of support on the trip.

● Let the parents and carers know about the shark topic from the beginning and encourage them to take the children to the library to look for story and information books about fish.

● Ask parents and carers to encourage the children to keep a lookout for fish that appear on the television and to record any sightings of fish in a local park lake, the sea or a river. Some families will have an aquarium at home, which they may allow small groups of children to visit. The record can be pictorial and/or have a written description, which the adults and children can create together.

● A member of the community may be keen on fishing or aquarium keeping and be willing to come and talk to the children about it.

● Ask the parents and carers if they have any model fish, or photographs that they would be willing to lend for display purposes.

➤ Make up a box of story and information books about fish (see Book bank, pages 74–75 for ideas).

➤ Provide several pairs of small binoculars and magnifying glasses.

Activity content

1   Refer to the concept map of the sea (see page 3) and see if the children can identify the names of any of the fish. They can then circle them on the map.

2   Look at the pictures of the sharks and other fish together and talk about their different colours, shapes and sizes.

3   Talk with the children about any experiences they have had of seeing fish in real life or on television. Encourage the children to describe what they saw and if they have held a fish to say what it felt and smelt like.

4   Look at a short nature video clip of life under the sea or of a story about a fish (see Book bank, pages 74–75).

5   Share a story or information book from the sea book box (see pages 74–75).

6   Talk about the different parts of a shark. As the children mention a part, draw it on a large piece of paper until all the parts are assembled. Talk about what each part does.

7   Talk about the differences between a shark and an octopus: body shape, tentacles, sharp teeth, eyes, scales, colour. Have some large clear pictures available to aid the comparison.

8   Make your visit to the Sea Life Centre or aquarium, drawing on the expertise of the staff or using your own prepared materials.

9   Have the magnifying glasses available for the children to use to watch the fish closely in the giant tanks.

10 Take photographs with the digital camera (see page 7) of the children looking around the Sea Life Centre or the aquarium.

11 View any film taken on the trip and print off the photographs for use in the sea display (see page 2).

12 Talk about nourishment that we can gain from eating fish and the various meals that can be made from them. Be sensitive to the feelings of any vegetarians in the group and suggest alternative means of gaining the nutrients present in fish.

Extending learning

Key questions

Q   Who has seen a fish? Can you tell us what it is like? Are they hot or cold? What do they feel like?

Q   Has anyone been fishing with a net or a rod? Can you tell us about it?

Q   Has anyone seen a fish on television? What did it look like?

Q   Does anyone have any fish in a tank at home? Could you bring your goldfish to show us, Katy? Or, perhaps we could visit your house, Amir, to see your aquarium?

Q   How is a shark different from an octopus? Can you describe them?

Q   What parts do most fish have? What do they use their tails and fins for? Do they need to breathe? What do they eat?

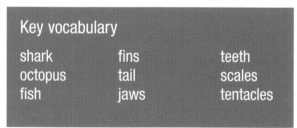

Key vocabulary

shark	fins	teeth
octopus	tail	scales
fish	jaws	tentacles

Follow-up activities

■   Cook fish fingers for a snack or lunch or make fish-shaped biscuits.

■   Make a fish with a paper plate. Cut out a wedge and staple it on the opposite side to form the fish's tail. Draw on an eye and decorate the fish by gluing on overlapping circles of different coloured tissue paper to form the scales. Stick the fish on the wall as part of the display or suspend them from the ceiling with thread.

■   Make an octopus from an upturned polystyrene cup painted green. When the paint is dry, add large black eyes with a felt-tip pen. To make the tentacles, punch eight holes round the bottom of the cup. Cut four green pipe cleaners in half and thread one end of each through each of the holes and secure. Add the models to the display and use them for props in storytelling sessions.

■ Visit a fishmonger's or the fish counter in the local supermarket to look at all the different textures, and experience the sea smells of the variety of cooked and uncooked fish.

2 Story: *The Great White Man-eating Shark*

This activity is based round a story by Margaret Mahy. It is a cautionary tale of a boy called Norvin who took advantage of the fact that he looked rather like a shark to frighten other people out of the sea, so that he could have it all to himself, until one day he meets a real shark who rather than wanting to eat him, wants to marry him!

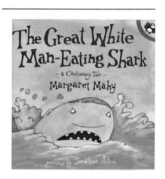

⬢ Links to the Foundation Stage Curriculum

PSE   Have a developing awareness of their own needs, views and feelings, and be sensitive to the needs, views and feelings of others.

CLL   Use vocabulary and forms of speech that are increasingly influenced by experience of books.

Adult:child ratio 1:8

⬢ Resources

✔ Picture of a shark
✔ Copy of *The Great White Man-eating Shark* by Margaret Mahy (see Book bank, page 74)
✔ White paper
✔ Black felt-tip pens
✔ Scissors, glue
✔ Grey card
✔ Belt

Preparation

➤ Choose a large picture of a shark.

➤ Acquire a copy of *The Great White Man-eating Shark*, and arrange a time for the story session.

Activity content

1   Read the story to the children several times. If you have bilingual children, arrange to have a staff member who speaks their first language, or a parent or carer, to read the story too, or to follow up with questions.

2   Encourage the children to describe the setting for the story, what happened and who the main characters are.

3   Talk with the children about the ways in which Norvin looked like a shark: small sharkish eyes, a pointed sharkish head, sharp sharkish teeth. Also, the fact that he soon learnt to swim very well like a shark.

4   Talk about what made Norvin angry and what he did about it. Ask the children about his plan and whether it was successful. Discuss why it was so successful. Encourage the children to imagine what it was like when the people thought that Norvin was a real shark. Talk about how they reacted.

5   Ask the children if they can understand how Norvin felt; whether they have ever felt frustrated because there were so many people wanting to do the same thing at the same time. This could provide the opportunity to talk about life together in the setting, the need to give each other personal space sometimes and to learn to take turns. Ask the children if they agree with what Norvin did and to consider what else he could have done.

6   Ask the children what happened at the end of the story and why Norvin was so scared of the real shark. Talk about what the people did to keep their bay safe from sharks and what Norvin did.

7   Talk about the fact that not all sharks would eat humans; indeed, Norvin tells people in the story that whale sharks and basking sharks are vegetarian. Some of the children in the setting might also be vegetarian, which could provide an opportunity for further exploration.

8   Help the children to cut out their own dorsal fin from the grey card and to strap it onto their back by taping it to a belt. The children can then play a version of 'What's the Time, Mr Wolf?' although in this case it would be 'What's the Time, Mr (or Mrs) Shark?' The children become little fish and creep up behind the child playing the shark, who turns round and says 'Two o'clock' or 'Ten o'clock', for example. Finally, he or she calls out 'Dinnertime!' and chases the little fish. The one who is caught becomes the shark for the next game.

Extending learning

Key questions

Q In what ways did Norvin look like a shark?

Q Why was Norvin so angry? Have you ever felt like that? What did you do? Can you tell us about it?

Q What can we do here when too many children want to play with the same thing?

Q What did Norvin decide to do? Did his plan work? Why was that?

Q What job did Mrs Scorpio do? What job did Mr Dorsey do?

Q Do you agree with what Norvin did? Why? Why not?

Q What happened to scare Norvin? Did everyone know what he had done? Were they angry with him? What did they do to keep their bay safe?

Q Do all sharks eat people? Is anyone here a vegetarian? What is your favourite food?

Q Have you ever been in trouble and needed help? What happened? Do you think Norvin will try that trick again?

Key vocabulary	
shark	Caramel Cove
dorsal fin	Mrs Scorpio
swimmers	Mr Dorsey
Norvin	

Follow-up activities

■ Explore the work of the coastguard, particularly in countries where there are more often sharks swimming near to the coast, such as Australia. Find out how they try to protect the swimmers and the surfers.

■ Make a pop-up card so that the shark's jaws over the centrefold show its sharp teeth when the card is opened (see Photocopiable sheet 4).

■ Learn the rhyme 'Four Little Fishes Swimming Out to Sea' by Glenda Banks (see Singing games and poems, page 75). Act out the rhyme with four little fish and one big shark. One little fish gets eaten by the shark, one hides in a great big shell, another chases after a wave and the last one goes back home to his mum...And that left none!

3 Make an ocean scene

This activity gives the children the opportunity to create their own ocean to add to the sea display. The children can personalise their own scene as they concentrate on their own choice of fish with distinct patterns and colour schemes.

Links to the Foundation Stage Curriculum

PD   Use simple tools to effect changes to the materials.

CD   Explore colour, texture, shape, form and space in two or three dimensions.

Adult:child ratio 1:8

● Resources

- ✔ Story from the book box
- ✔ Pictures of fish
- ✔ Empty cardboard boxes (about shoebox size)
- ✔ A4 card
- ✔ Felt-tip pens
- ✔ Brown, green and blue paint
- ✔ Thread
- ✔ Scissors
- ✔ Hole puncher, hole reinforcements
- ✔ Variety of tissue and cellophane paper
- ✔ Glue
- ✔ Stapler
- ✔ Fish-shaped sponges

● Preparation

- ➤ Set aside a table area covered with an oilcloth.
- ➤ Gather together the resources listed above.
- ➤ Choose an ocean story from the book box.

● Activity content

1 Read the chosen ocean story and talk about the environment where fish live. What their needs are: food, shelter, unpolluted water, protection.

2 Stand the box on its side and encourage the children to paint the bottom brown on the inside to look like the muddy seabed, the other three sides blue or green to simulate the sea, and set it aside to dry.

3 Look at the pictures of the fish together and ask the children to consider which ones they are going to include in their scene. To encourage the children to study the fish carefully, play a game with them. Ask one child to think of a fish and to begin to describe it while the others try to guess which one it is he or she is thinking of.

4 Encourage the children to draw their own designs on their A4 card.

5 The fish shapes can then be cut out and decorated with strips of coloured paper or with the felt-tip pens on both sides. Although only one side will be visible most of the time, the fish may spin round on their thread. Strips of paper can be stapled on very effectively to create the fins and the tail of a fish.

6 Punch a hole in the middle of each fish's upper back and reinforce the hole to prevent the card from tearing. Put thread through the hole and tape the ends to the roof of the box, so the fish are suspended against the background of the seawater.

7 The process is then repeated with a different kind of fish.

8 Large stones can be added to simulate rocks and small stones, shells can be placed on the ocean bed and strips of green tissue can be used to represent weed floating in the water.

Extending learning

Key questions

Q What is the sea like as a place to live? What do the fish need to eat? How can they protect themselves? Where can they hide?

Q What happens to them if the water is polluted? How does it become like this? Can we do anything to help?

Q Who can describe one of the fish in this picture? How big is it? What shape is it? What colour is it? Why did you choose it?

Q Which colour will you choose for the bottom of the sea? Why?

Q Which colour will you choose for the water? Green or blue?

Q Can you draw a fish and cut it out? Which colours do you want for your fish?

Q What does this fish feel like? Is it hot or cold? Is it smooth or rough? What patterns can you see? Is it long and thin? Is it flat with a stubby nose? Has it got spikes or long wavy tentacles?

Key vocabulary		
large	green	smooth
middle-sized	pattern	long
small	zigzag	thin
paint	wavy	flat
blue	spiky	tentacles
brown		

Follow-up activities

- Having gone through the process once, the materials can be kept available for the children to make other fish designs, and to try different methods. For example, sponges in the shape of fish can be used for printing in different colours.

- Learn and repeat simple rhymes (see Singing games and poems, page 75) such as:

> Dance for your Daddy my little laddie
> Dance for your Daddy my little lamb
> You shall have a fishy
> On a little dishy
> You shall have a fishy
> When the boat comes in

> One, two, three, four, five,
> Once I caught a fish alive
> Six, seven, eight, nine, ten
> Then I let it go again
> Why did you let it go?
> Because it bit my finger so
> Which finger did it bite?
> This little finger on the right

Encourage independent learning

Creative area

Additional resources

- ✔ Picture of a boat sailing on the sea for the children to study
- ✔ Triangular and trapezium shapes
- ✔ Pencils
- ✔ Scissors
- ✔ A4 paper and coloured card
- ✔ Blue, green and white paint
- ✔ Small yellow and white circles of sticky paper
- ✔ Cotton wool or white tissue paper
- ✔ Straws
- ✔ Small sponges

Possible activities/learning outcomes

KUW Show curiosity, observe and manipulate objects.

To make a picture of a sailing boat on a sea alive with fishes:

Give the children an A4 sheet of paper to colour to create the sea by applying a mixture of blue and green paint with a small sponge.

While the paint is drying, provide a trapezium for the children to draw round on the A4 card and cut out to make a simple boat shape, which can then be stuck onto the paper. Triangular shapes can be used in the same way to create the sails, which may be decorated in any way the children wish before being added to the picture. A mast can be made from a straw and a flag stuck in the top. White cotton wool or tissue paper added under the prow simulates waves breaking against the boat as it moves through the water.

A yellow circle for the sun or a white one for the moon can be added. Seagulls can be painted in the sky circling the boat, and fishes drawn, cut out and stuck in the sea.

The practitioner role

- ▲ Provide the resources and be ready to add to these as the children's play develops.
- ▲ Encourage the children to wonder what it would be like to sail out far away to sea. What adventures would they like to have?
- ▲ Share the story of Borka (see Book bank page 74), who sailed away with a boat by mistake.

Water area

Additional resources

- ✔ Water tray
- ✔ Model sharks and other fish (see Equipment, page 75)
- ✔ Boats, nets
- ✔ Magnetic tape or paper clips
- ✔ Balsa wood rods with a small magnet on the end
- ✔ Thread for a fishing line

Possible activities/learning outcomes

KUW Talk about what is seen and what is happening.

Add rubber models of sharks and other fish to the water tray. Use some of the boats for fishing vessels and provide nets to throw out to trawl the fish.

Attach magnetic tape or a paper clip to the back of the fish's neck and 'catch' them with a magnet tied to the end of a balsa wood rod and line or embedded in the end of the stick.

Play a game to follow up where fish made from card, and then laminated, can be 'caught' from a sea of crumpled blue activity paper in a similar way, and placed on a lotto board (alternatively, see Equipment, page 75).

The practitioner role

▲ Provide the resources for the activities, and be prepared to add others as the children develop their own ideas.

▲ Encourage the children to talk about what they are doing and what they have found out about the strength of the magnets. Ask whether they can lift all the fish.

▲ Talk about any experiences the children have had of fishing and read some related stories and poems from the book box (see page 65 and Singing games and poems, page 88.)

Book bank

Information books

Life-size Sharks: And Other Underwater Creatures by David Bergen (2005). Chrysalis Children's Books. ISBN 1844584232

Fishy Tales (DK Readers) (2003). Dorling Kindersley. ISBN 0751343986

Sherston 123-CD by Simon Hosler and Bill Bonham. www.sherston.com (3–6yrs). One activity with fish.

Sharks (Oxford Reds Series) by Chris Powling (2000). Oxford University Press. ISBN 0199106231

Under the Sea (Usborne Beginners Series) (2004). Usborne Publishing. ISBN 0746045433

Under the Sea (Chunky Board Books) by F. Watt (2004). Usborne Publishing. ISBN 0746062869

Websites

Amazon: www.amazon.co.uk (*Fish* from the Eyewitness Series). An insight into fish from the coral reefs to the deepest oceans.

Amazon: www.amazon.co.uk (*Shark* and *Ocean* video from the Dorling Kindersley Eyewitness Series). Two programmes on one video.

Baker Ross: www.bakerross.co.uk

Disney Educational Productions: http://dep.disney.go.com/educational (*Sharks* video)

Early Learning Centre: www.elc.co.uk

Fisher Price: www.fisher-price.com/uk

Library Video: www.libraryvideo.com (*Deep Sea Dive*) (45 minutes)

One Poster: www.oneposter.com sharks/seahorses/blue ocean wildlife

Reflections on Learning: www.reflectionsonlearning.co.uk

Sea Life Centres: www.sealifeeurope.com Situated in Blackpool, Birmingham, Brighton, Great Yarmouth, Scarborough and Weymouth.

Sherston: www.sherston.com

The Ninja Corporation: www.thepopupco.com

Story books

Commotion in the Ocean by Giles Andreae and illustrated by David Wojtowycz (1998). Orchard Books. ISBN 184121101X. Written in rhyme.

There's an Octopus Under My Bed by Dawn Apperley (2001). Bloomsbury. ISBN 0747550239

Where the Forest Meets the Sea by Jeannie Baker (1998). Walker Books. ISBN 0744563011

The Hidden Forest by Jeannie Baker (2005). Walker Books. ISBN 0744578760

Dougal's Deep-sea Diary by Simon Bartram (2004). Templar Publishing. ISBN 1840115084

Borka: The Adventures of a Goose with No Feathers by John Burningham (1999). Red Fox. ISBN 0099400677

Freddy Fish (Inflatable Bath Book) illustrated by Sonia Canals (2000). Pinwheel Children's Books. ISBN 1902249984. Story written on the fins.

Mister Seahorse by Eric Carle (2004). Puffin Books. ISBN 0141380896

Goldfish and Chrysanthemums by Andrea Cheng and illustrated by Michelle Chang (2003). Lee and Low Books. ISBN 1584300574 (5–8yrs)

Finding Nemo. Video available from Blockbuster. Tel: 08456 060 999

Fidgety Fish by Ruth Galloway (2001). Little Tiger Press. ISBN 1854307533. Limpets that clung, jellyfish that stung.

Smiley Shark by Ruth Gallaway (2003). Little Tiger Press. ISBN 1854308629

Starfish (Baby Bathtime Series) picture credits Frank Greenaway, Stephen Oliver and Dave King (2004). DK Publications. ISBN 0751337722. Plastic pages in a starfish shape.

The Great White Man-eating Shark by Margaret Mahy (1995). Puffin Books. ISBN 0140554246

Two Funny Fish (Collins Big Cat Series) by Michaela Morgan and illustrated by Jon Stuart (2005). Collins Educational. ISBN 0007185804

The Dance of the Eagle and the Fish by Aziz Nesin and illustrated by Kağan Güner (2001). Milet Publishing. ISBN 1840593164

Way Down Deep in the Deep Blue Sea by Jan Peck and illustrated by Valerie Petrone (2004). Pocket Books. ISBN 0743489845

The Rainbow Fish by Marcus Pfister and translated by J. Alison James (1992). North-South Books. ISBN 1558580093. The rainbow fish shares out his glittering scales.

Fish (Living Nature Series) by Angela Royston (2005). Chrysalis Children's Books. ISBN 1844583813

Shark in the Park! by Nick Sharratt (2002). David Fickling Books. ISBN 0385604696 (Foundation Stage, Key Stage 1)

The Very Silly Shark (Peek-a-Boo Pop-ups) by Jack Tickle (2004). Little Tiger Press. ISBN 1854309994 (not suitable for under 3yrs). In rhyming couplets.

The Turtle and the Island by Barbara Ker Wilson and illustrated by Frané Lessac (1990). Frances Lincoln. ISBN 0711206244

Maui and the Big Fish by Barbara Ker Wilson and illustrated by Frané Lessac (2004). Frances Lincoln. ISBN 0711221693 (5–8yrs)

Singing games and poems

'Four Little Fishes Swimming Out to Sea' by Glenda Banks in *This Little Puffin: A Treasury of Nursery Rhymes, Songs and Games* compiled by Elizabeth Matterson (1991). Puffin Books. ISBN 0140340483

Seaside Poems edited by Jill Bennett and illustrated by Nick Sharratt (1998). Oxford University Press. ISBN 0192761749

'Skate' by Alan Brownjohn in *Happy Landings: Poems for the Youngest* (Zebra Books) edited by Howard Sergeant (1971). Evans Bros. ISBN 0237351897

'Three Jellyfish' by Jean Chadwick in *This Little Puffin: A Treasury of Nursery Rhymes, Songs and Games* compiled by Elizabeth Matterson (1991). Puffin Books. ISBN 0140340483

'Going Fishing in the Deep Blue Sea' by Alison Wells and Elizabeth Matterson (1991) in *This Little Puffin: A Treasury of Nursery Rhymes, Songs and Games* compiled by Elizabeth Matterson. Puffin Books. ISBN 0140340483

Equipment

Mini Sticky Sea Creatures. Throw them at any surface and they will crawl down and return to their original shape and size. Assorted designs. www.bakerross.co.uk Tel: 0870 241 1867 (5yrs +)

Nature Tub Series. Sixteen assorted 4cm ocean animals. www.bakerross.co.uk Tel: 0870 241 1867 (3yrs +)

Counting Fish 'N' Net. Scoop and strain the water with three fish to catch. www.cradleandall.co.uk/shop (see Toys and Playtime section, accessed 15/08/2005) Tel: 01767 600601 (12mths +)

Magnetic Fishing. Using fishing rods to catch fish and pick up points. www.elc.co.uk Tel: 08705 352 352 (3yrs +)

Octopus Activity Centre. Floating activity centre with suction pads to attach to bath. Allows for scooping, pouring, rainmaking and squirting. www.elc.co.uk Tel: 08705 352 352 (12mths +)

PowerTouch Books. Rescue heroes. www.elc.co.uk Tel: 08705 352 352 (5yrs +)

Sea Turtle Model. www.elc.co.uk Tel: 08705 352 352 (3yrs +)

Stingray Model. www.elc.co.uk Tel: 08705 352 352 (3yrs +)

Under the Sea. A vinyl book featuring sea creatures and a big squeak! www.elc.co.uk Tel: 08705 352 352 (12mths +)

Aquaria. One hundred and sixty eight pieces with a range of reusable stickers that allow children to create an underwater scene with creatures and jewellery. www.fisher-price.com/uk Tel: 01628 500303 (5yrs +)

Ocean Wonders Aquarium. Sea sounds, entertaining lights and bubbles, and a range of sea creatures such as fish and opening clams with interactive features. www.fisher-price.com/uk Tel: 01628 500303 (birth +)

Mirror Exploratory. Rectangular with mirrored internal surfaces; items placed within it are reflected back from the rear mirror and multiplied many times in the end mirrors. www.reflectionsonlearning.co.uk Tel: 01732 225850

Airflow Adventure: Undersea Adventure. Four pods (an octopus, a liner, a pirate ship and a shark) linked by four tunnels. It inflates in 60 seconds and is very large. www.thepopupco.com Tel: 0151 495 1677 (3–9yrs)

Seal

Links to the Foundation Stage Curriculum

Follow-up Activities

Home–setting Links

Seal

Extending Learning

Resources and Preparation

Activity Content

Adult-led focus activities

1 Observation

Most of the creatures in the sea are small, but some are huge. While some rays and sharks are the biggest fish, there are mammals, too, that have to come to the surface to breathe. Among these sea mammals are seals, walruses and whales. We tend to think of dolphins as being a separate group on their own, but they are, in fact, a group of small whales. Many kinds of seals live in cold seas and they have a thick layer of fat called blubber under their skin to keep them warm. The flippers that they have developed instead of legs mean that they make slow progress on land, but are very fine swimmers and can move very quickly once they get into the water. The sea is the seal's hunting ground where it searches for fish to feed on.

⬡ Links to the Foundation Stage Curriculum

CLL Talk activities through, reflecting on and modifying what they are doing.

KUW Find out about, and identify, some features of living things, objects and events they observe.

> Adult:child ratio
> 1:2 for a zoo visit;
> 1:8 for a video clip

⬡ Resources

- ✔ Zoo to visit
- ✔ Pictures of seals and other sea mammals
- ✔ Stories and information books about seals and other sea mammals (see Book bank, page 88)
- ✔ Model and toy seals (see Equipment, page 88)
- ✔ Binoculars
- ✔ Large sheet of paper with a felt-tip pen
- ✔ Digital camera and/or video camera
- ✔ Paper and writing utensils
- ✔ Mirrors

⬡ Preparation

> If your setting is within an appropriate distance from a zoo, make a preparatory visit to inspect the facilities and to find out if there are any appropriate activities already provided for the age group of your children, and if not, decide on some activities of your own devising.

➤ Collect a number of video and film clips involving seals and other sea mammals to show to the children. Video clips from nature programmes, such as those broadcast by David Attenborough for the BBC with hidden cameras, can show the life cycles of various sea mammals including seals (see Websites, page 88).

➤ Collect pictures and posters of seals and other sea mammals (see Websites, page 88).

➤ Arrange a date for the zoo visit and make the booking with the organisation concerned and with your transport providers.

⬢ Home–setting links

● Write letters to the parents and carers about the trip to make it clear what is happening and what is needed in terms of funds, food and offers of support on the trip.

● Let the parents and carers know about the seal topic from the beginning and encourage them to take the children to the library to look for story and information books about seals and other sea mammals.

● Ask parents and carers to encourage the children to keep a lookout for seals that appear on the television or that they see on holiday. The record can be pictorial and/or have a written description, which the adults and children can create together.

● Ask the parents and carers if they have any model seals or other sea mammals, or pictures that they would be willing to lend for display purposes.

➤ Make up a box of story and information books about seals and other sea mammals (see Book bank, page 88 for ideas).

➤ Provide several pairs of small binoculars.

⬢ Activity content

1 Refer to the concept map of the sea (see page 3) and see if the children can identify the names of any of the sea mammals. They can then circle them on the map.

2 Look at the pictures of the seals and the other sea mammals together and talk about their different colours, shapes and sizes. Talk about how they breathe and what they like to eat.

3 Talk with the children about any experiences they have had of seeing seals in real life or on television. Encourage the children to describe what they saw and what they think a seal's skin feels like.

4 Look at a short nature video clip of life under the sea or of a story about a seal (see Websites, page 88).

5 Share a story or information book about seals from the sea book box (see above).

6 Talk about the different parts of a seal. As the children mention a part, draw it on a large piece of paper until all the parts are assembled. Talk about what each part does.

7 Make your visit to the zoo, drawing on the expertise of the staff or using your own prepared materials.

8 Have the binoculars available for the children to use to watch the seals closely in the giant waterways. Zoos usually post up times when the seals are being fed, so try to be in the vicinity for this activity.

9 Take photographs with the video and/or digital camera (see page 7) of the children looking at the seals.

10 Talk to the children about the sounds that the seals make.

11 Talk about the way the seals are able to clap with their flippers. Clap some rhythms for the children to copy.

12 View any film taken on the trip, and print off the photographs for use in the sea display (see page 2).

13 Remind the children of the talk you had in your session on sharks about the nourishment that they can gain from eating fish, and the various meals that can be made from them (see page 66). Talk about the fact that seals eat fish.

14 Talk about the similarities and differences between a seal and a shark: warm blooded and cold blooded, the way their babies are born, the way they breathe, the food they eat.

15 Introduce other sea mammals such as dolphins, whales and walruses and talk about their features.

Extending learning

Key questions

Q Who has seen a seal? Where did you see it? Can you tell us what it looked like? What was it doing? Do you think that it would feel hot or cold if you touched it? What do think its skin feels like?

Q What parts do seals have? What do they use their tails and flippers for? Do they need to breathe? What do they eat?

Q How is a seal different from a shark? How is a seal the same as a shark? Can you describe them?

Q Have you seen seals performing any tricks? Can you clap this rhythm?

Q What sound do the seals make? Does it sound like any other animals?

Q What other sea mammals do you know? Can you describe them?

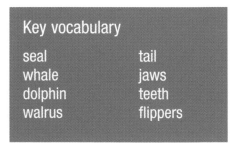

Key vocabulary

seal	tail
whale	jaws
dolphin	teeth
walrus	flippers

Follow-up activities

■ Set up a seascape using mirrors to reflect the water and the sea mammals. This can be set up using a cardboard box with mirrors taped to the internal sides, or a commercial product is on the market (see Equipment, page 88). Blue paper covered with bubble wrap and cellophane can simulate the sea and model sea mammals can be played with in the 'water' (see Equipment, page 88). Large stones can be used for rocks for those mammals that are able to come out of the water to bask in the sun.

■ Make a seal book of your own using the pictures taken at the zoo with the digital camera. Decide on the text on each page with the children. This can be written underneath the picture or on the opposite page. Choose one picture for the front cover and the title. Mount and laminate the photographs and the text before stapling the pages together, or punching holes in them to slot into a small ring binder.

2 Story: *Baby Seal All Alone*

Baby Seal is feeling very lonely because she has to play all on her own. There are plenty of exciting sea creatures all around her, but they are very big and her parents are afraid that she will get hurt. One day, however, Mother and Father Seal have a new baby and Baby Seal is no longer lonely.

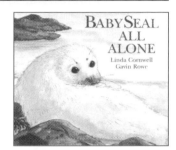

Links to the Foundation Stage Curriculum

PSE Show a strong sense of self as a member of different communities, such as their family and setting.

CLL Show awareness of rhyme and alliteration.

MD Count actions or objects that cannot be moved.

Adult:child ratio 1:8

Resources

✔ Copy of *Baby Seal All Alone* by Linda Cornwell and illustrated by Gavin Rowe (see Book bank, page 88)
✔ Sheets of A3 paper with a felt-tip pen

Preparation

➤ Gather together the resources as indicated above.
➤ Arrange a storytelling session for a small group of children.

Home–setting links

● Let the parents and carers know about the seal topic from the beginning and encourage them to take the children to the library to look for books about seals and other sea mammals.
● If you have bilingual children, arrange for a member of staff, or a parent or carer who shares their first language, to tell the story in that language to all the children.
● If any families have model seals at home, ask if these can be brought in to the setting to show the children.

Activity content

1 Recall your experience of the zoo visit. Encourage the children to share their own versions of watching the seals feeding. Ask them to describe what they saw and how it felt. Talk about the way the seals move on land and in the sea.

2 Arrange for the story of *Baby Seal All Alone* to be read in English, and any other appropriate languages, pointing out the details of the seal and how it is similar to and different from the other animals in the story: in its shape, its colours, its way of moving, its food. Compare the seal to other sea mammals, such as a walrus and a dolphin.

3 Identify the main characters in the story and describe what they are doing. Encourage the children to copy these actions.

4 Count the number of animals featured in the story.

5 Talk about how Baby Seal felt when she could not play with anyone. Ask the children if they have ever felt lonely and what happened.

6 Ask the children if they can think of any games they would like to play with the Baby Seal. Make a list of the ideas on the A3 sheet of paper, and encourage the children to illustrate them as you go.

7 Ask the children about the ending and about their own brothers and sisters. Encourage them to share the experiences they have shared with their brothers and sisters.

Extending learning

Key questions

Q What did you see at the zoo when it was time for the seals to be fed? What did they have to eat? How did they get to the food? How did they move on the land? How did they move through the water?

Q How is a seal similar to a walrus? What features are different? How is a seal similar to a dolphin? What features are different? How is a seal similar to a whale? What features are different?

Q Can you think of a name for Baby Seal that alliterates with 'seal'? Can you think of a sea creature that alliterates with your name? For example, Darren Dolphin, Waquas Whale, Lucy Lobster, Shamin Shark.

Q What other characters are in the story besides Mother, Father and Baby Seal? How many are there? What were they doing? Can you move like that? What have the seal, the eagle and the polar bear in common? How is the reindeer different?

Q How did Baby Seal feel when she could not play with the other creatures? Have you ever felt like that? What happened?

Q What games would you like to play with Baby Seal?

Q Have you any brothers and sisters? What games do you play together? How did Baby Seal feel when she saw the new baby?

Key vocabulary	
seal	eagle
Mother Seal	whale
Father Seal	a polar bear
Baby Seal	reindeer

Follow-up activities

- Keep the copy of *Baby Seal All Alone* available on the sea display for the children to look at any time.
- Learn the action rhyme:

    Slippery Sam was a slippery seal
    And a slippery seal was he;
    He slithered and slid to the sandy shore
    Then he slipped back into the sea.

    (See Singing games and poems, page 88.)

- The children can pull themselves along on the carpet using their bent arms as flippers. When they pass a certain spot, they reach the sea, at which point they stand up and run with their arms still bent to simulate flippers. This activity enables the children to relate to the theme in a completely different way. Action songs give children the opportunity to repeat words and rhymes in a fun way; it teaches them the need to listen carefully and to express themselves with others.
- Place the book box with stories and rhymes about seals and other sea mammals where the children can access it easily.

3 Make a model seal

Seals make the ideal creatures to model from clay because they have smooth coats and very few intricate features. If grey clay is used, then it can stay this colour to represent the grey seals. If brown clay is used, then the models can be painted black once they have dried.

Links to the Foundation Stage Curriculum

MD Sustain interest for a length of time on a pre-decided construction or arrangement.

KUW Select the tools and techniques they need to shape, assemble and join materials they are using.

Adult:child ratio 1:6

Resources

- ✔ Brown and grey clay
- ✔ Wooden tools
- ✔ Black paint, brushes
- ✔ Clay boards
- ✔ Fishing line

✔ Scissors, staples
✔ Sticky labels
✔ Old black and grey socks
✔ Tissue paper
✔ Paper streamers
✔ Wool
✔ Ribbons
✔ Felt-tip pens

⬡ Preparation

➤ Gather together the resources above in sufficient quantities for each child to make a grey and a black seal.

➤ Arrange for a model making session with six children seated around a large table with aprons on and sleeves rolled up.

➤ Put an oilcloth on the table before setting out the boards.

⬡ Activity content

To make a clay seal:

1 Look at a picture of a seal and talk about the parts of its body.
2 Begin by kneading a piece of clay into a smooth round shape.
3 Roll the clay in your hands until it is smooth and malleable.
4 Gradually pull out the tail at the back and divide it at the end.
5 Bend the body into an upright position.
6 Gently pull the flippers out from each side of the seal at the bottom of its body.
7 Pull its head gently into a pointed nose at the end.
8 Take the wooden tool and make holes for the eyes and draw in some lines along the ends of the flippers and along the tail.
9 Cut some short lengths of fishing line, or other fine thread, and push them into the clay on either side of the nose to simulate whiskers.
10 Set the seal aside to dry and repeat the process with a second piece of clay.
11 When the brown clay is dry, paint it black and leave it to dry.
12 Place the seals on the sea display.

⬡ Extending learning

Key questions

Q Which are the main parts of the seal's body?
Q What should the seal's skin look like? Should it be rough or smooth?
Q What shape should the tail be?
Q Can you pull the seal's body upright?
Q Where should the flippers be formed?

Q What shape will the seal's head be? Its nose?

Q How could you make the eyes? How could you make the patterns to show the divisions on its flippers and its tail?

Key vocabulary	
ball of grey clay	tail
ball of brown clay	flippers
body	eyes
head	whiskers
nose	

Follow-up activities

■ Make a seal puppet with an old black or grey sock. Cut big round eyes from some white sticky labels and colour in the central part black leaving a thin white rim round the edge. Stick these onto the foot of the sock. Use lengths of fishing line to weave through the sock below the eyes for the whiskers. Cut out some flipper shapes from grey or black activity paper and staple these on halfway down the sock on the outside. Cover the staples with sticky tape to protect your hand. Put your hand in the sock and rest your wrist on the table. Now you are ready to act out some of the stories and rhymes from your book box (see page 79).

■ Read *Dougal's Deep-sea Diary* (see Book bank, page 88). Make some pictures of merpeople. Talk to the children about these mythical creatures, which they will come across in many stories, who live under the sea and who have the upper bodies of people and the lower bodies of fish. Some will have seen the Disney version of *The Little Mermaid* and you could show part of this film on a video (see Websites, page 88). Allow the children freedom to design their merpeople as they wish. Provide coloured tissue paper for scales, blue activity paper to form the backing, paper streamers, wool or ribbons for their hair and felt-tip pens to draw the more delicate features of their faces.

Encourage independent learning

Malleable materials

Additional resources

- ✔ Clay and/or dough
- ✔ Copy of *Baby Seal All Alone*
- ✔ Pictures of a variety of Arctic sea creatures
- ✔ Wooden tools
- ✔ White and black paint

Possible activities/learning outcomes

MD Use appropriate shapes to make representational models or more elaborate pictures.

Make some dolphins, walruses and whales with the clay and add these to the display. The children may want to go on to make the eagle, the polar bear and the reindeer from the story, as well as the new baby seal so they can re-enact the narrative.

When the models are hard, paint the creatures appropriately, using the story as a reference, or the models of those particular creatures (see Equipment, page 88).

When the paint is dry, encourage the children to develop their own stories and rhymes using these characters. Warn the children that their models might not be as robust as their plastic counterparts if they are using them as props.

The practitioner role

- ▲ Provide pictures and/or models of the creatures for the children to study alongside the copy of *Baby Seal All Alone*.
- ▲ Provide the other resources identified above and be ready to add others as the children's play develops.
- ▲ Discuss the physical characteristics of the creatures with the children, and talk about their different shapes. Use the vocabulary that the children might need; for example, *long*, *thin*, *sharp*, *smooth*, *hard*, *soft*, *heavy*. Talk about how they can get the effect they want by using the modelling tools.
- ▲ Talk with the children about which basic colours are needed for each creature and how they can mix the other colours that they need.

Creative area
Additional resources

- ✔ Digital camera
- ✔ Computer and printer
- ✔ Laminator
- ✔ A4 paper
- ✔ A4 thick coloured card
- ✔ Pens, thick black felt-tip pens
- ✔ Glue, scissors
- ✔ Resealable food bags (medium)
- ✔ Sticky address labels

Possible activities/learning outcomes

MD Match some shapes by recognising similarities and orientation.

Use the digital camera to photograph the merpeople pictures designed by the children.

Print off the pictures from the computer onto A4 copy paper.

Stick the paper onto A4 thick coloured card.

Draw clear black lines on the back of the card in the shape of jigsaw pieces (the number will depend on the age and skill of the children).

Laminate the sheets.

Cut along the black lines and shuffle the pieces.

Each child can put together his or her own jigsaw and then try other people's puzzles.

Store the pieces of each puzzle in resealable plastic food bags, and label them by getting the child to write the title of the puzzle; for example, 'Katy's merman', or 'Leroy's mermaid' on the sticky label. The children might want to add a second label giving the number of pieces.

Add the puzzles to your resources.

The practitioner role

▲ Take photographs of the merpeople pictures designed by the children or help the children to use the digital camera themselves.

▲ Assist the children in printing off the pictures from the computer onto A4 copy paper.

▲ Support the children as they stick the merpeople pictures onto the card.

▲ Demonstrate how to draw the black lines on the back of the card in the shape of jigsaw pieces. Talk to the children about the number of pieces they want.

▲ Laminate the sheets for the children.

▲ Involve the children, as far as they are able, in cutting along the lines.

▲ Having supported the children in the process of making the jigsaw puzzle, encourage them to talk through the stages as they go along, to describe their design and to say why they chose it.

▲ Arrange for the puzzles to be stored safely, but remain accessible to the children.

Book bank

Information books

Seal (My Little Animals) by Barron's (2000). Barron's Educational Series. ISBN 0764152394. Board book.

Surfer the Seal (Baby Animals Growing Up) by Jane Burton (1989). Gareth Stevens Publishers. ISBN 0836802101

Whales and Dolphins (Kingfisher Young Knowledge Series) by Caroline Harris (2005). Kingfisher Books. ISBN 0753410699

A Harbour Seal Pup Grows Up (Baby Animals Series) by Joan Hewett, Richard Hewett (photographer) (2001). Carolrhoda Books. ISBN 1575051664

Baby Seal (Nature Babies) by Aubrey Lang, Wayne Lynch (photographer) (2004). Fitzhenry & Whiteside. ISBN 1550417266

In the Ocean (Nature Trails) (Touch and Feel Book) by Maurice Pledger and A. J. Wood (2001). Silver Dolphin. ISBN 1571454535

Websites

Disney Educational Productions: http://dep.disney.go.com/educational (*Seals* video)

Early Learning Centre: www.elc.co.uk

One Poster: www.oneposter.com seals/dolphins/whales

Story books

Harpo: The Baby Harp Seal by Patricia Arrigoni (1995). Travel Publishers International. ISBN 0962546887

Shark Goes Zoom! (Bang on the Door Series) (2003). Oxford University Press. ISBN 0192725661

Dougal's Deep-sea Diary by Simon Bartram (2004). Templar Publishing. ISBN 1840115084

Mermaids (Touchy-Feely Board Books Series) by S. Cartwright and F. Watt and illustrated by G. Bird (2004). Usborne Publishing. ISBN 074605663X

Baby Seal All Alone by Linda Cornwell and illustrated by Gavin Rowe (2000). Little Tiger Press. ISBN 1854306022

Kotik: The Baby Seal by Angele Delaunois and Fred Bruemmer (photographer) (1995). Orca Book Publishers. ISBN 1551430509

The Snail and the Whale by Julia Donaldson and illustrated by Axel Scheffler (2003). Macmillan Children's Books. ISBN 033398224X

Splash! by Jane Hissey (2003). Red Fox. ISBN 9099447975. Splash is a baby seal who rescues a teddy bear.

Fergus the Sea Dog by Tony Maddox (2004). Piccadilly Press. ISBN 1953407194

Sea Creatures Make Friends with Sam Seal by Jane Massey (2000). Silver Dolphin. ISBN 1571454179. Meet his new friends and fit them into the pages to complete the story – touch and fit.

Sglod at Sea (Pont Hoppers) by Ruth Morgan and illustrated by Suzanne Carpenter (2001). Pont. ISBN 185902937X

Dolphin Boy by Michael Morpungo and Michael Foreman (2004). Anderson Press: ISBN 184270320X

Rainbow Fish and the Big Blue Whale by Marcus Pfister (1998). North-South Books. ISBN 0735810095

The Whale's Song by Dyan Sheldon (1997). Penguin Books. ISBN 0140559973

Ebb and Flo and the Baby Seal by Jane Simmons (2005). Orchard/Watts Group. ISBN 1843628406

Sailing Boat (Slide-Along-the-Slot-Books) by Helen Stephens (2003). Macmillan Children's Books. ISBN 0333968271

Singing games and poems

'Slippery Sam Was a Slippery Seal' by Anon. in *This Little Puffin: A Treasury of Nursery Rhymes, Songs and Games* compiled by Elizabeth Matterson (1991). Puffin Books. ISBN 0140340483

Song of the Whale by Anon. in *Happy Landings: Poems for the Youngest* (Zebra Books) edited by Howard Sergeant (1971). Evans Bros. ISBN 0237351897

Seaside Poems edited by Jill Bennett and illustrated by Nick Sharratt (1998). Oxford University Press. ISBN 0192761749

Equipment

Great White Whale Model. www.elc.co.uk Tel: 08705 352 352 (3yrs +)

Lightweight Binoculars. Magnification to the factor of six. www.elc.co.uk Tel: 08705 352 352 (3yrs +)

Wind-Up Dolphin. www.elc.co.uk Tel: 08705 352 352 (12mths +)

Photocopiable sheets

Photocopiable sheet 1
(See activity on page 9.)

Match the shape

A spiral

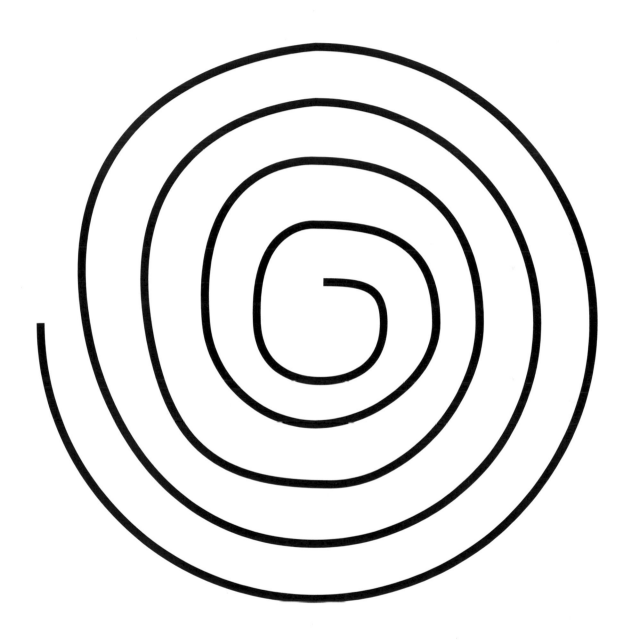

A seagull mask

1 Cut out the head, the eyes and the nose from thin white card. Punch out and reinforce the two small holes.

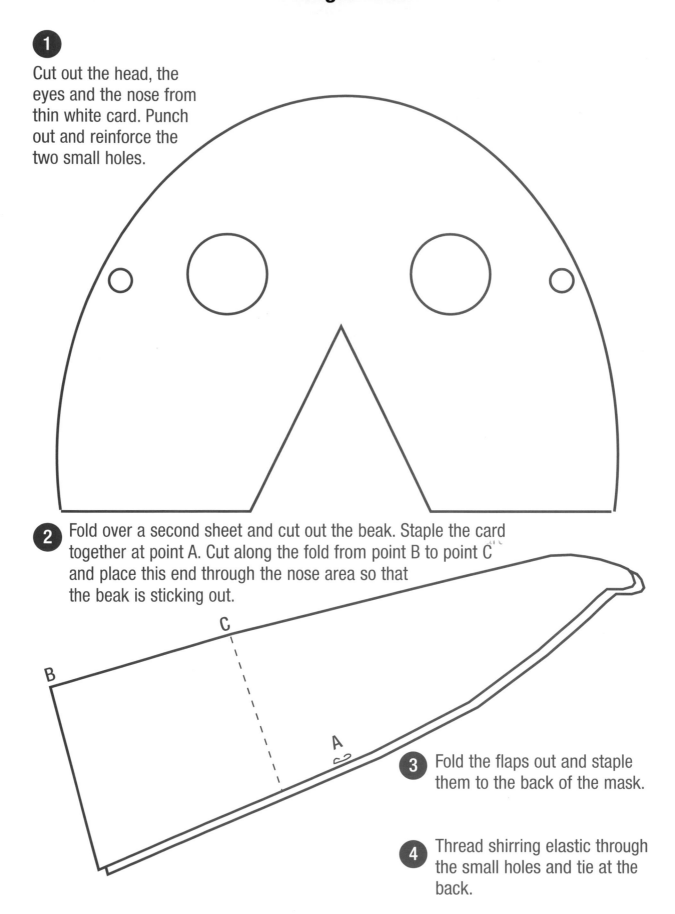

2 Fold over a second sheet and cut out the beak. Staple the card together at point A. Cut along the fold from point B to point C and place this end through the nose area so that the beak is sticking out.

3 Fold the flaps out and staple them to the back of the mask.

4 Thread shirring elastic through the small holes and tie at the back.

A shark pop-up card

1

Take two A5 sheets of activity paper and fold each one in half.

2

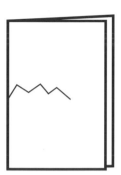

Draw a zigzag line from the folded edge and cut along it with scissors.

3

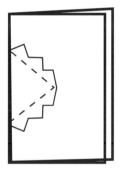

Fold back the flaps. Press along the fold lines.

4

Open the flaps and the whole paper. Push the flaps inwards to form the shark's mouth and draw its body round the mouth.

5

Glue the second piece of paper to the first avoiding the mouth area.

6

Colour the inside of the mouth black. Decorate the outside of the card as you wish.